G000293610

EYEWITNESS TRAVEL

ISTANBUL

POCKET GUIDE

LONDON, NEW YORK,
MELBOURNE, MUNICH AND DELHI
www.dk.com

This edition produced by Silva Editions Ltd.,
233 Woodcote Road, Purley, Surrey CR8 3PB

PROJECT EDITOR Sylvia Goulding

ART EDITOR Paula Keogh

RESEARCH AND INDEX Mike Goulding

CARTOGRAPHER John Plumer

Conceived by Redback Publishing,
25 Longhope Drive, Farnham, Surrey GU10 4SN.

Reproduced by Colourscan (Singapore)

Printed and bound by Leo Paper Products Ltd, China

First published in Great Britain in 2007
by Dorling Kindersley Limited
80 Strand, London WC2R 0RL

Reprinted with revisions 2009

Copyright 2007, 2009 © Dorling Kindersley Limited, London

A Penguin Company

A CIP CATALOGUE RECORD IS AVAILABLE FROM THE BRITISH LIBRARY.

ISBN 978 1405 342 41 4

> **We're trying to be cleaner and greener:**
>
> • we recycle waste and switch things off
> • we use paper from responsibly managed
>   forests whenever possible
> • we ask our printers to actively reduce
>   water and energy consumption
> • we check out our suppliers' working
>   conditions – they never use child labour
>
> **Find out more about our values and
> best practices at www.dk.com**

**The information in this
DK Eyewitness Travel Guide is checked regularly.**
Every effort has been made to ensure that this book is up-to-date as
possible at the time of going to press. Some details, however, such as
telephone numbers, opening hours, prices, gallery hanging
arrangements and travel information, are liable to change. The
publishers cannot accept responsibility for any consequences arising
from the use of this book, nor for any material on third-party websites,
and cannot guarantee that any website address in this book will be a
suitable source of travel information. We value the views and
suggestions of our readers highly. Please write to:
Publisher, DK Eyewitness Travel Guides,
Dorling Kindersley, 80 Strand, London WC2R 0RL.

Carpet shops in Çorlulu Ali Paşa Courtyard

CONTENTS

The Blue Mosque, one of the most famous mosques in the world

Central Istanbul

This guide divides central Istanbul into four distinct areas, each with its own chapter. Three areas are south of the Golden Horn: Seraglio Point, a raised promontory with the sumptuous Topkapı Palace; Sultanahmet with two architectural masterpieces: Haghia Sophia and the Blue Mosque; and the Bazaar Quarter, a maze of narrow streets filled with commerce. North of the Golden Horn is cosmopolitan Beyoğlu.

The Galata Bridge *spans the Golden Horn between the Bazaar Quarter and Beyoğlu. In the background, the superb Süleymaniye Mosque can be seen (see p37).*

The Grand Bazaar *Myriad booth-like shops, under impressive painted vaults, offer a paradise of earthly goods for sale (see p40).*

Haghia Sophia *This mosque in Sultanahmet, one of the world's great architectural feats, was built in AD 537 as a Byzantine church (see pp26–7).*

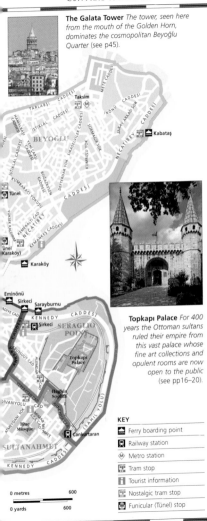

The Galata Tower *The tower, seen here from the mouth of the Golden Horn, dominates the cosmopolitan Beyoğlu Quarter (see p45).*

Topkapı Palace *For 400 years the Ottoman sultans ruled their empire from this vast palace whose fine art collections and opulent rooms are now open to the public (see pp16–20).*

KEY

🛳	Ferry boarding point
🚆	Railway station
Ⓜ	Metro station
🚊	Tram stop
ℹ	Tourist information
🚋	Nostalgic tram stop
🚠	Funicular (Tünel) stop

0 metres — 600
0 yards — 600

Istanbul's Highlights

Istanbul has a treasure trove of magnificent sights, ranging from mosques, palaces and museums to bazaars and Turkish baths. All the most famous sights are central and close together, but a visit to the Asian shore is also well worth while.

Fatih Mosque

Mosques and Churches

Haghia Sophia
One of the world's greatest feats of architecture, Haghia Sophia dates from AD 537 (*see pp26–9*).

The Blue Mosque
So named after its stunning blue İznik tilework, made at the peak of tile production, the Blue Mosque is Istanbul's best-known landmark (*see pp30–31*).

Süleymaniye Mosque
Sinan, the greatest Ottoman imperial architect, built this mosque in honour of his patron, Süleyman the Magnificent (*see p37*).

Fatih Mosque
Rebuilt after an earthquake, this mosque was founded by Mehmet the Conqueror after his conquest of the city. It has an especially fine courtyard (*see p55*).

Church of St Saviour in Chora
Several cycles of beautiful Biblical mosaics and some fine frescoes adorn this Byzantine church, now a mosque (*see p59*).

Markets

Grand Bazaar
The largest market in the world, the Grand Bazaar contains about 4,000 shops in a roofed labyrinth of passages (*see p40*).

Book Bazaar
A wealth of printed documents, academic tomes and other printed matter is for sale here (*see p40*).

Wednesday Street Market
One of the city's colourful neighbourhood markets is right next to the Fatih Mosque and everything from fresh produce to household goods and bulbs is on sale here (*see p55*).

Spice Bazaar
The Spice Bazaar is an exotic trading house for dried herbs, spices and other foodstuffs, laid out in colourful heaps and patterns (*see p36*).

Galatasaray Fish Market
Istanbul's best fish market, selling fresh fish from the Sea of Marmara, constantly sprinkled with water to keep them cool (*see p44*).

Grand Bazaar

Dolmabahçe Palace

Palaces

Aynalı Kavak Palace
This secluded, airy and intimate palace shows subtler aspects of Ottoman taste. It also houses a collection of Turkish musical instruments *(see p65)*.

Şale Pavilion
One of a group of buildings in the leafy Yildiz Park built by 19th-century sultans. It has some 50 splendid rooms, including the Mother-of-Pearl Salon *(see p63)*.

Dolmabahçe Palace
This opulent 19th-century palace is home to such marvels as 2-m (7-ft) high vases, a Baccarat crystal staircase and an alabaster bathroom *(see p64)*.

Beylerbeyi Palace
The imperial summer palace was built in the 19th century to entertain visiting dignitaries. Its subtle beauty can be appreciated from the Bosphorus *(see p70)*.

Topkapi Palace
This huge but also fairly restrained Baroque palace was used as the official royal residence for 400 years. The treasury contains a myriad of treasures and precious objects such as jewel-encrusted thrones *(see pp16–20)*.

Museums

Archaeological Museum
The exhibits in this superb museum range from prehistory to the Byzantine era, including the Alexander Sarcophagus, a marble tomb depicting the Greek hero, and a tablet with the world's oldest surviving peace treaty *(see p14)*.

Statue in the Archaeological Museum

Museum of Calligraphy
On display here are examples of the finest calligraphic works, some produced by sultans, as well as the tools for creating them *(see p39)*.

Museum of Turkish and Islamic Arts
Magnificent carpets, glassware and ceramics bear witness to Turkey's rich artistic heritage. Also exhibited is a fully recreated yurt *(see p28)*.

Mosaics Museum
One of the floors from the Great Palace is exhibited here, a stunning mosaic depicting hunting scenes, making this a fascinating museum to visit *(see p25)*.

Military Museum
One of the highlights here is the Mehter band which used to accompany the sultans on their campaigns and which still performs there today *(see p65)*.

The Flavours of Istanbul

Thanks to its varied climates, Turkey is one of the few countries that is able to grow all its own food. Freshness is the hallmark of its varied cuisine, drawn from the many cultures that were subject to nearly five centuries of Ottoman rule.

The Anatolian steppe

The steppe stretching from Central Asia to Anatolia is one of the oldest inhabited regions of the world. Dishes from this vast area are as varied as the ethnic groups that live here. Turkey's most famous culinary staples, yogurt, flat bread and the kebab, originate in this region. The use of fruits, such as pomegranates, figs and apricots, in Turkish savoury dishes stems from Persian influences, north of the steppe. From the Middle East, further south, nomads introduced the fiery blast of chili. Its use was once an essential aid to preserving meat in the searing desert heat.

Pomegranates

Ottoman cuisine

It was in the Topkapı Palace kitchens that mouth-watering dishes to rival French cuisine evolved at the height of the Ottoman Empire, in the 16th and 17th centuries. Ottoman rule expanded, and flavours from far-flung places were absorbed. Complex dishes of stuffed meats and vegetables, with such fanciful names as "lady's lips" and "the Imam fainted", appeared. This imperial tradition lives on in dishes such as *karni-yarik* (aubergines stuffed with minced lamb, pine nuts and dried fruit) and *hünkar beğendili köfte* (meatballs served with a smoked aubergine purée).

Chicken şiş kebab
Lamb şiş kebab
Chilli sauce
Stuffed aubergine
Prawn kebab
Lamb cutlet
Doner kebab

A selection of typical Turkish kebabs and accompaniments

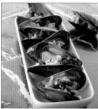

Midye dolması *Mussels stuffed with a spicy rice mixture, steamed and served with lemon juice*

Local dishes and specialities

Istanbul's location on the sea means that fresh fish is readily available. In the winter months especially, there is a bounty of oily fish in the Bosphorus, such as bluefish, bonito tuna, sea bass, mullet and mackerel, waiting to be reeled in. From the Black Sea, Istanbul is also well provided with a steady supply of juicy mussels and *hamsi*, a type of anchovy. Sweets are also popular and eaten throughout the day, not just after a meal. Istanbul is renowned for its *baklava*, sweet pastries coated with syrup and often filled with nuts.

KNOW YOUR FISH

The profusion of different species in the waters around Istanbul make the city a paradise for fish lovers:

Barbunya Red mullet
Çupra Sea bream
Dilbaliği Sole
Hamsi Anchovy
Kalamar Squid
Kalkan Turbot
Kefal Grey mullet
Kiliç Swordfish
Levrek Sea bass
Lüfer Bluefish
Midye Mussels
Palamut Bonito Tuna
Uskumru Mackerel

Fresh catch from the Bosphorus on a fish stall in Karaköy

Levrek pilakisi *Sea bass fillets simmered with potatoes, carrots, tomatoes, onions and garlic*

Kadayif *Rounds of shredded filo pastry stuffed with nuts and doused with honey*

A Glossary of Mezes

Mezes, Turkish starters, are served in all Turkish restaurants. There are hundreds of different kinds, often accompanied by rakı. Most mezes are served cold, and very few of them contain fish or meat, making them ideal for vegetarians.

Zeytinyağlı enginar

Çoban salatası

Ayse fasulye

Melon with beyaz peynir

Tarama

Turkish breads

Bread is the cornerstone of every meal in Turkey and comes in a wide range of shapes and styles. Mezes are eaten with bread and traditionally washed down with rakı (a clear, anise-flavoured spirit).

Ekmek
Basic crusty white loaf, the most common bread.

Yufka
The typical bread of nomadic communities, made from thinly rolled sheets of dough which are cooked on a griddle and dried to help preserve them. They can then be heated up and served hot.

Pide
The type of flat bread that is usually served with mezes and kebabs in restaurants. It consists of a flattened circle or oval of dough that is baked in an oven. It may be brushed with beaten egg and sprinkled with sesame seeds or black cumin. It is a staple during many religious festivals. In the month of Ramadan, no meal is considered to be complete without plenty of *pide*.

Simit
A crisp, ring-shaped savoury loaf that usually comes covered in sesame seeds.

A selection of Turkish breads

A selection of cold mezes

Cold mezes

A Turkish meal begins with a selection of appetizing starters known as mezes, which are placed in the middle of the table for sharing. In a basic *meyhane* restaurant, you may be offered only olives, cheese and slices of melon, but in a grander establishment the choice of mezes can be enormous and may include hot and cold dishes.

Humus
Chickpea purée flavoured with sesame paste, garlic, oil and lemon juice.

Tarama
A dip made with cod's roe, garlic and olive oil.

Zeytinyağli enginar
Artichokes cooked in olive oil.

Ayse fasulye
Green beans with tomato sauce.

Beyaz peynir
A creamy, feta-like cheese, often served with melon.

Fasulye Piyazi

Patlıcan salatası
Smoked aubergine salad.

Çoban salatası
Tomato, red onion and cucumber salad.

Haydari
A dip made with thick yoghurt, flavoured with garlic, herbs and spices.

Fava
Purée of broad beans.

Lakerda
Finely sliced smoked tuna served with lemon.

Fasulye piyazı
A salad of haricot beans with olive oil and lemon juice, sometimes topped with egg.

Böreks and dolmas

Hot mezes

Although most mezes are cold, there is usually also a small number of hot starters available. Anything that can be stuffed is made into a *dolma*, for example vine leaves, peppers and mussels. *Börek* (or *böreği*) are deep-fried savoury pastries, filled with mince, spinach or cheese with herbs.

Sigara böreği
Cigar-shaped pastries.

Muska böreği
Triangular pastries.

Yalancı yaprak dolması
Stuffed vine leaves.

Midye dolması
Mussel shells stuffed with rice.

SERAGLIO POINT

On the hilly, wooded promontory where the Golden Horn, the Sea of Marmara and the Bosphorus meet stands the grandiose Topkapı Palace, the residence of the Ottoman sultans and the women of the harem for 400 years. Adjacent to it is the renowned Archaeological Museum.

SIGHTS AT A GLANCE

Museums and Palaces
Archaeological Museum **2**
Topkapı Palace pp16–20 **1** ✱

Mosques and Churches
Haghia Eirene **3**

Historic Buildings and Monuments
Fountain of Ahmet III **4**
Sirkeci Station **8**

Streets and Courtyards
Cafer Ağa Courtyard **6**
Soğukçeşme Sokağı **5**

Turkish Baths
Cağaloğlu Baths **7**

SEE ALSO
• *Street Life p21.*

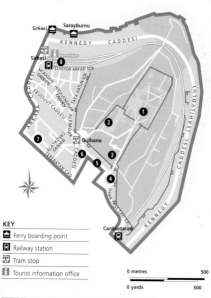

KEY

🚢 Ferry boarding point

🚆 Railway station

🚋 Tram stop

ℹ Tourist information office

| 0 metres | | 500 |
| 0 yards | | 500 |

◀ *The Courtyard of the Black Eunuchs at Topkapi Palace*

Glazed frieze of a bull from Ishtar Gate, Babylon

Topkapı Palace ❶

See pp16–20.

Archaeological Museum ❷

Map H5. Osman Hamdi Bey Yokuşu. Open Tue–Sun (some sections may close in winter). Adm charge.

Although the collection was begun only in the 19th century, the museum now holds a vast number of items spanning over 5,000 years, from figurines modelled in the 3rd millennium BC to Turkish pottery thrown in the 19th century.

Geometric Period Cypriot Jug

Classical Archaeology

This collection includes the highlights of the museum: the breathtaking sarcophagi from the royal necropolis at Sidon in today's Lebanon. They are thought to have been made for Phoenician kings who ruled during the 6th–4th centuries BC.

Istanbul through the Ages

Among the exhibits are a bronze snakehead from the Serpentine Column and iron chains that were hung across the Bosphorus by the Byzantines to stop hostile ships.

Museum of the Ancient Orient

Star exhibits in this section are the artifacts from early Mesopotamia (present-day Iraq), including glazed brick friezes from the Ishtar Gate, Babylon's main entrance.

Anatolia and Troy

A recreated Anatolian royal tomb contains cooking utensils and wooden furniture. The Troy section traces the excavation of nine civilizations in the Asian city.

Other Collections

Other sections focus on Turkish tiles and ceramics; Anatolia's neighbouring cultures; Thracia, Bithynia and Byzantine; and there is also a Children's Museum.

Haghia Eirene ❸

Map H6. First courtyard of Topkapı Palace. Free.

This 6th-century Byzantine church has three unique features: the synthronon (five rows of built-in seats for clergymen); an icono-clastic black mosaic cross on a gold background; and a cloister-like courtyard where deceased emperors once lay in their porphyry sarcophagi. Most have been moved to the Archaeological Museum.

Fountain of Ahmet III

Fountain of Ahmet III ❹

Map H6. Junction of İshak Paşa Cad & Babıhümayun Cad. Free.

The most beautiful of Istanbul's fountains (1728), this delicate Turkish Rococo fountain has five small domes, mihrab-shaped niches and dizzying floral reliefs. Ottoman "fountains" do not spout jets of water, but are more like ornate public taps. Each of this fountain's four walls is equipped with a tap, or *çeşme*, above a carved marble basin. Elaborate inscriptions by the 18th-century poet Seyit Vehbi Efendi honour the fountain and its founder.

Soğukçeşme Sokağı ❺

Map H6.

Charming old wooden houses line this narrow, sloping cobbled lane ("the street of the cold fountain"), which squeezes between the outer walls of Topkapı Palace and the towering minarets of Haghia Sophia. Traditional houses like these were built in the city from the late 18th century onwards. Renovated in the 1980s, some of the buildings are now attractive pastel-painted guesthouses, and one has been converted to house a library of histori-cal writings on Istanbul and an archive of engravings and photographs of the city.

Cafer Ağa Courtyard ❻

Map G6. Caferiye Sok. Open daily. Free.

This peaceful courtyard at the end of an alley was built in 1559 by Sinan for the chief black eunuch, as a *medrese* (theological college). Sinan's bust still presides over the tranquil café that occupies the courtyard today. The former students' cells are now used by calligraphers, jewellers and other artisans selling their wares.

An example of calligraphy for sale at Cafer Ağa Courtyard

Topkapı Palace ①

Mehmet II's palace, his main residence, was built in 1459–65 as a series of pavilions within four vast courtyards, to mirror the tented Ottoman encampments. The seat of government until the 16th century, the palace was opened to the public in 1924.

Harem *The labyrinth of exquisite rooms where the sultan's wives and concubines lived can be visited on a guided tour (see p20).*

Exhibition of Arms and Armour

Gate of Salutations: entrance to the palace

Divan *The viziers of the imperial council met in this chamber, sometimes watched covertly by the sultan.*

Second Courtyard

The Gate of Felicity *is also called the Gate of the White Eunuchs.*

The kitchens *contain an exhibition of ceramics, glass and silverware.*

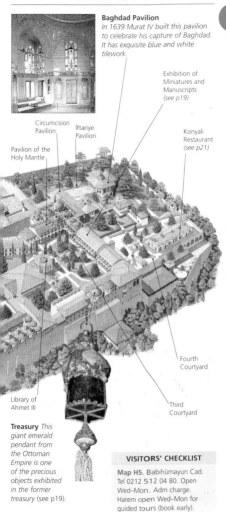

Baghdad Pavilion
In 1639 Murat IV built this pavilion to celebrate his capture of Baghdad. It has exquisite blue and white tilework.

Exhibition of Miniatures and Manuscripts
(see p19)

Circumcision Pavilion

Iftariye Pavilion

Pavilion of the Holy Mantle

Konyalı Restaurant
(see p21)

Fourth Courtyard

Library of Ahmet III

Third Courtyard

Treasury This giant emerald pendant from the Ottoman Empire is one of the precious objects exhibited in the former treasury (see p19).

VISITORS' CHECKLIST

Map H5. Babıhümayun Cad. Tel 0212 512 04 80. Open Wed–Mon. Adm charge. Harem open Wed–Mon for guided tours (book early).

Exploring the Palace's Collections

During their 470-year reign, the Ottoman sultans amassed a glittering collection of treasures. After the foundation of the Turkish Republic in 1923, this was nationalized and the bulk of it put on display in Topkapı Palace.

Ceramics, Glass and Silverware

The palace kitchens contain a vast display of Chinese porcelain, second best only to China itself, and, to a lesser extent, Japanese objects. Brought to Turkey along the Silk Route, the Chinese porcelain on display spans four dynasties, from the 10th to the 20th centuries. It includes early celadon, made to look like jade, and exquisite blue-and-white pieces, mostly of the Ming era. Ottoman craftsmen were heavily influenced by Chinese porcelain, particularly at their fledgling ceramics industry at İznik. The old confectioners' pantry displays huge cauldrons once used to feed 12,000 palace residents and guests.

Arms and Armour

Taxes and tributes from all over the empire were once stored in this chamber, which was known as the Inner Treasury. Straight ahead as you enter are a series of horse-tail standards. Carried in processions or displayed outside tents, these proclaimed the rank of their owners. Viziers, for example, merited three, while the grand vizier five, while the sultan's banner would flaunt nine. The weaponry includes ornate swords, bows made by some sultans themselves, 15th-century Ottoman chainmail and colourful shields. Next to such exquisite items, the huge iron swords used by European crusaders look crude by comparison.

Beautiful carafes from the palace's extensive silver collection

Imperial Costumes

A collection of imperial costumes is displayed in the Hall of the Campaign Pages, whose task was to look after the royal wardrobe. It was a palace tradition that on the death of a sultan his clothes were carefully folded and placed in sealed bags. As a result, it is possible now to see a perfectly preserved kaftan once worn by Mehmet the Conqueror. The reforms of Sultan Mahmut II included a revolution in the dress code. The end of an era came as plain grey serge replaced the earlier luxurious silken textiles.

Treasury

The Treasury holds thousands of glittering precious and semi-precious stones. Among its star exhibits in the four halls are: Mustafa III's diamond-encrusted ceremonial chainmail; a pearl statuette of a seated prince, sent to Sultan Abdül Aziz from India; the splendid Topkapı dagger (1741), a gift meant for the Shah of Persia, who died before it reached him; bejewelled plumes for imperial turbans; the 86-carat Spoonmaker's diamond; the gold-plated Bayram throne given to Murat III by the Governor of Egypt in 1574; and bones said to be from John the Baptist's hand.

The Topkapı dagger

A miniature, depicting the Council of Ministers, 1588

Miniatures and Manuscripts

The palace has over 13,000 miniatures and manuscripts, among them depictions of warriors and fearsome creatures known as *Demons and Monsters in the Life of Nomads*, by Mohammed Siyah Qalem, possibly from the 12th century. Also on show are fine examples of calligraphy, including texts from the Koran.

Clocks

European clocks given to, or bought by, various sultans form the majority of this collection. They range from simple, weight-driven 16th-century examples to an exquisite 18th-century English mechanism encased in mother-of-pearl and featuring a German organ which played tunes on the hour to the delight of the harem.

Topkapı Palace: The Harem

The word Harem comes from the Arabic for "forbidden". It was the residence of the sultan's wives, concubines and children, guarded by black slave eunuchs. At one time, over 1,000 concubines lived in the Harem. The last women left in 1909.

The Cage

The sultan's brothers were confined to rooms known as the Cage, to avoid succession contests.

Paired Pavilions

A star sight, these twin apartments, built in the 17th century for the crown prince, boast superb İznik tiles and a dome lined with gilded canvas.

Stained-glass window in the Paired Pavilions

Dining Room of Ahmet III

The walls of this 18th-century chamber, also known as the Fruit Room, are painted with sumptuous fruit and flowers.

Imperial Hall

The largest room in the Harem, this hall was used for entertainments. Against one wall stands a throne, from which the sultan viewed the events.

Courtyard of the Black Eunuchs

Marble columns line this courtyard, which still has some old-fashioned, wrought-iron lamps.

Salon of the Valide Sultana

The sultan's mother, the valide sultana, was the most powerful woman in the Harem and had some of the best rooms.

The Imperial Hall, the largest room in the Harem

Corridor leading into the Cağaloğlu Baths

Cağaloğlu Baths ❼

Map G6. Prof Kazım İsmail Gürkan Cad 34, Cağaloğlu. Open daily. Free.

These sumptuous Turkish baths, built by Sultan Mahmut I in 1741, have separate men's and women's sections. Each section consists of three parts: a *camekan*, a *soğukluk* and the main bath chamber or *hararet*, which centres on a massive octagonal massage slab. The staff are happy to explain the procedure. Even if you do not wish to sweat it out, you can still take a look inside the entrance corridor and the *camekan* of the men's section or relax with a drink by the fountain.

Sirkeci Station ❽

Map G5. Sirkeci İstasyon Cad, Sirkeci. Open daily. Free.

This superb railway station, built to receive the Orient Express, was officially opened in 1890, although the luxurious train had been running into Istanbul for a year by then. The design, by the German architect Jasmund, successfully combines Byzantine alternating stone and brick courses with a Seljuk-style monumental recessed portal and Muslim horseshoe arches around the windows. Trains from this station serve Greece and the European part of Turkey. Istanbul's other main railway station is on the Asian shore.

STREET LIFE

FOOD

Konyalı
Map H5. Topkapı Palace, Sultanahmet. Tel 0212 513 96 96. **Moderate**
A gastronomic landmark, serving mezes and fish as well as international dishes in a superb setting, inside the Topkapı Palace, overlooking the Sea of Marmara.

Sarnıç
Map H6. Soğukçeşme Sok, Sultanahmet. Tel 0212 512 42 91. **Expensive**
Underground restaurant, converted from a Byzantine cistern, cool in summer. Wrought-iron chandeliers, fireplace and candles, plus piano music for dinner. Various menu options.

CAFÉS

Orient Express Café
Map G5. Sirkeci Train Station, Sirkeci, Eminönü.
Located next to Platform 1, this café offers a limited but satisfying menu, dominated by lamb dishes, in an historic location. A good place in which to escape the bustle.

See p80 for price codes.

SULTANAHMET

This area gets its name from Sultan Ahmet I, who built the Blue Mosque, a superb example of early Byzantine architecture. It faces Istanbul's other main monument, Haghia Sophia. A square alongside marks the site of a Roman stadium. Tradional-style houses line a maze of alleyways.

SIGHTS AT A GLANCE

Mosques and Churches

Blue Mosque pp30–31 **6** ✸
Church of SS Sergius and Bacchus **13**
Haghia Sophia pp26–7 **1** ✸
Sokollu Mehmet Paşa Mosque **12**

Museums

Mosaics Museum **5**
Museum of Turkish and Islamic Arts **7**
Vakıflar Carpet Museum **4**

Squares and Courtyards

Hippodrome **8**

Historic Buildings and Monuments

Basilica Cistern **2** ✸
Baths of Roxelana **3**
Bucoleon Palace **14**
Cistern of 1,001 Columns **9** ✸
Constantine's Column **11**
Tomb of Sultan Mahmut II **10**

SEE ALSO

• Street Life p33.

KEY

🚋 Tram stop

🛈 Tourist information office

| 0 metres | 400 |
| 0 yards | 400 |

◀ The elegant domes of the Blue Mosque

Hagia Sophia ➊

See pp26–7.

Basilica Cistern ➋

Map G6. 13 Yerebatan Cad.
Open daily. Adm charge.

This vast underground water
cistern, a beautiful piece
of Byzantine engineering,
is the most unusual tourist
attraction in the city. The
cavernous vault was laid out
under Justinian in 532, on
the site of an earlier cistern,
to satisfy the growing
demands of the Great Palace
on the other side of the
Hippodrome *(see p28–9)*.
For a century after the conquest, the Ottomans did not
know of the cistern's exist-
ence. It was rediscovered
after people were found
to be collecting water, and
even fish, by lowering buck-
ets through holes in their
basements. The cistern's
roof is held up by 336 columns, each over 8 m (26 ft)
high. Only about two-thirds
of the original structure is
visible today, the rest has
been bricked up. Two
columns rest on Medusa heads,
plundered by the Byzantines
from earlier monuments.

The Baths of Roxelana

Baths of Roxelana ➌

Map G/H6. Ayasofya Meydanı,
Sultanahmet. Open Wed–Mon.
Free. Under restoration.

These baths were built for
Süleyman the Magnificent
by Sinan, and are named
after Roxelana, the sultan's
scheming wife. They were
designated for the use of the
congregation of Haghia
Sophia when it was used as
a mosque. With the women's
entrance at one end of the
building and the men's at the
other, their absolute symme-
try makes them perhaps the
most handsome baths in the
city. The building is now
a government-run carpet
shop, but the baths' original
features are still clearly visible. A look around it is a
must for those who have no
intention of baring them-
selves in a public bath, but
are curious about what the

Interior of the Basilica Cistern

interior of a Turkish baths is like. Each end starts with a *camekan*, a massive domed hall which would originally have been centred on a fountain. Next is a small *soğukluk*, or intermediate room, which opens into a *hararet*, or steam room. The hexagonal massage slab in each *hararet*, the *göbek taşı*, is inlaid with coloured marble, a sign of imperial origin.

Vakıflar Carpet Museum

Map G7. Imperial Pavilion, Blue Mosque, Sultanahmet. Open Tue–Sat (closed 2009 for restoration). Closed for public & religious hols. Adm charge.

A ramp to the left of the main doorway into the Blue Mosque *(see pp30–31)* leads up to the Vakıflar Carpet Museum, installed in what was formerly the mosque's imperial pavilion. This pavilion was built by Ahmet I and used for Friday prayers. The carpets are protected from the destructive sunlight by stained-glass windows.

Dating from the 16th to the 19th centuries, they are mostly from the western Anatolian regions of Uşak, Bergama and Konya. Mosques have played a vital role in the preservation of early rugs: all the carpets in this museum lay inside mosques until recently.

Mosaics Museum ❺

Map G7. Arasta çarşısı, Sultanahmet. Open Tue–Sun. Adm charge.

This museum was created simply by roofing over a part of the Great Palace of the Byzantine Emperors, discovered in the 1930s. In its heyday the palace had hundreds of rooms, many with gold mosaics. The surviving late 5th-century AD floor mosaic shows wild and domestic beasts and includes some hunting and fighting scenes. It is thought to have adorned the colonnade leading from the royal apartments to the imperial enclosure beside the Hippodrome.

Detail of a 5th-century floor mosaic in the Mosaics Museum

Haghia Sophia ❶

Over 1,400 years old, Haghia Sophia, the "Church of Holy Wisdom", is one the world's greatest and most influential architectural monuments. The Ottomans converted it into a mosque in the 15th century, adding minarets, tombs and fountains.

Byzantine Frieze
Among the ruins of the entrance to the earlier Haghia Sophia (AD 415) is this frieze of sheep.

Calligraphic Roundel

Buttresses

Inner Narthex

The Galleries
were originally used by women during services.

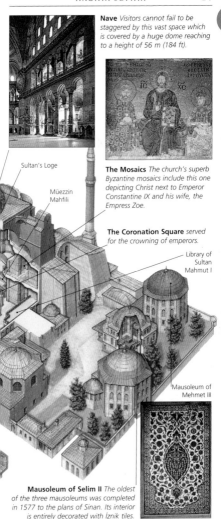

Nave *Visitors cannot fail to be staggered by this vast space which is covered by a huge dome reaching to a height of 56 m (184 ft).*

The Mosaics *The church's superb Byzantine mosaics include this one depicting Christ next to Emperor Constantine IX and his wife, the Empress Zoe.*

Sultan's Loge

Müezzin Mahfili

The Coronation Square *served for the crowning of emperors.*

Library of Sultan Mahmut I

Mausoleum of Mehmet III

Mausoleum of Selim II *The oldest of the three mausoleums was completed in 1577 to the plans of Sinan. Its interior is entirely decorated with İznik tiles.*

Recreated yurt interior, Museum of Turkish and Islamic Arts

Blue Mosque **6**

See pp30–31.

Museum of Turkish and Islamic Arts **7**

Map G6. Atmeydanı Cad. Open Tue–Sun. Adm charge.

Over 40,000 items are on display in the former palace of İbrahim Paşa (c.1493–1536), the most gifted of Süleyman's many grand viziers. The collection was begun in the 19th century and ranges from the earliest period of Islam through to modern times. Each room focuses on a different chronological period or geographical area of the Islamic world.

The museum is renowned for its collection of rugs.

These range from 13th-century Seljuk fragments to the palatial Persian silks that cover the walls from floor to ceiling in the palace's great hall. An ethnographic section focuses on the lifestyles of different Turkish peoples, particularly the nomads of central and eastern Anatolia. Here the exhibits include recreations of a round felt yurt (Turkic nomadic tent) and a traditional brown tent.

Hippodrome **8**

Map G6.

Little is left of the gigantic stadium which once stood here. Originally laid out by Emperor Septimus Severus in the 3rd century AD and enlarged by Emperor

Constantine, it held up to 100,000 people. The site is now a public garden.

There are some remains that give a sense of its scale. The road running around the square almost directly follows the line of the chariot racing track. Constantine adorned the stadium with obelisks and columns, of which three remain. The beautifully carved Egyptian Obelisk (1500 BC) is broken and is probably only one third of its original height. The 4th-century base depicts Theodosius I in various situations. The Serpentine Column next to it, believed to date from 479 BC, was shipped here from Delphi. The heads of the serpents were knocked off in the 18th century by a drunken Polish nobleman. One such head is on display in the Archaeological Museum *(see p14)*. The Column of Constantine Porphyrogenitus (date unknown) is named after the emperor who restored it in the 10th century.

Cistern of 1,001 Columns ⑨

Map G6. İmran Öktem Cad 4. Adm charge.

This 4th century cistern is the second largest in the city, spanning an area of 64 m (210 ft) by 56 m (185 ft). The herring-bone brick roof vaults are held up by 224 marble columns – not 1,001. Filled with rubble until recently, the cistern has now been transformed into a modern shopping complex.

Tomb of Sultan Mahmut II ⑩

Map G6. Divanyolu Cad, Çemberlitaş. Open daily. Free.

This large octagonal mausoleum was built in 1838, the year before Sultan Mahmut II's death, and is shared by sultans Mahmut II, Abdül Aziz and Abdül Hamit II. Within, Corinthian pilasters divide up walls which groan with symbols of prosperity and victory. The huge tomb dominates the cemetery.

The Egyptian Obelisk and the Serpentine Column in the Hippodrome

Blue Mosque ❻

One of the most famous religious buildings in the world, the mosque was commissioned by Sultan Ahmet I and built from 1609 to 1616 by Mehmet Ağa, the imperial architect. Its six minarets were initially considered an affront against Mecca.

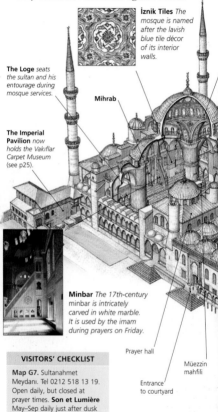

İznik Tiles *The mosque is named after the lavish blue tile décor of its interior walls.*

The Loge *seats the sultan and his entourage during mosque services.*

Mihrab

The Imperial Pavilion *now holds the Vakıflar Carpet Museum (see p25).*

Minbar *The 17th-century minbar is intricately carved in white marble. It is used by the imam during prayers on Friday.*

Prayer hall

Entrance to courtyard

Müezzin mahfili

VISITORS' CHECKLIST

Map G7. Sultanahmet Meydanı. Tel 0212 518 13 19. Open daily, but closed at prayer times. **Son et Lumière** May–Sep daily just after dusk (see board on Mlnar Mehmet Ağa Caddesi for details). Free.

Inside of the Dome
Mesmeric designs, employing flowing arabesques, are painted onto the interior of the mosque's domes and semidomes.

View of the Domes *The graceful cascade of domes and semidomes makes a striking sight when viewed from the courtyard below.*

Over 250 windows flood the mosque with light.

Ablutions Fountain
The hexagonal şadırvan is now purely ornamental since ritual ablutions are no longer carried out at this fountain.

The Courtyard *covers the same area as the prayer hall, balancing the building.*

Washing the Feet
Taps outside the mosque permit the concluding ritual ablution of the feet.

Interior of the 16th-century Sokollu Mehmet Paşa Mosque

Constantine's Column **11**

Map F6. Yeniçeriler Cad, Çemberlitaş. Open daily. Free.

Built in AD 330 to celebrate the new Byzantine capital, the 35 m- (115 ft-) high column originally bore a statue of Emperor Constantine. Its base is supposed to have included Noah's axe, Mary Magdalen's flask of anointing oil, and remains of the loaves of bread with which Christ fed the multitude.

Sokollu Mehmet Paşa Mosque **12**

Map F7. Şehit Çeşmesi Sok, Sultanahmet. Open daily. Free.

This mosque, built by the architect Sinan in 1571–2, is admired for the elegant design on its sloping site. Inside, the wall around the carved mihrab is covered in sumptuous green-blue İznik tiles, complemented by six stained-glass windows. A small greenish stone above the entrance is said to be from the Kaaba, the holy stone at the centre of Mecca.

Church of SS Sergius and Bacchus **13**

Map F7. Küçük Ayasofya Cad. Open daily. Free.

This decorative church, built in 1527 by Emperor Justinian and his wife, Theodora, is one of the city's most charming edifices. The two saints were Christian martyrs in Rome credited by Justinian with saving his life. The marble columns, the tracery of the capitals and the carved frieze above the columns are original. It was converted into a mosque in 1453.

Bucoleon Palace **14**

Map G7. Kenndey Cad. Free.

A creeper-clad section of stonework behind ancient sea walls and three windows framed in marble are what remains of the Bucoleon Palace, a maritime residence and part of the Great Palace. The ruined tower was a lighthouse. To get there, take the path under the railway from the Church of SS Sergius and Bacchus, turn left along Kennedy Caddesi for 400 m (450 yards). The site is unsafe to visit alone.

Wall of Bucolean Palace, part of the Byzantine Great Palace

STREET LIFE

RESTAURANTS

Turquoise
Map H7. Akbıyık Cad 40, Sultanahmet. Tel 0212 517 37 50. **Cheap**
Friendly, good value Turkish eatery decorated in Byzantine style. Good choice of mezes, köfte and kebabs. The grills are particularly recommended.

Sultanahmet Köftecisi
Map G6. Divanyolu Cad 12. Tel 0212 520 05 66. **Cheap**
Modest place but highly recommended for its köfte (meatballs). Much imitated, this is the original.

Türkistan Aşevi
Map G7. Tavukhane Sok 36. Tel 0212 638 65 25. **Cheap**
Converted Ottoman house, furnished with exquisite carpets and textiles. Guests are given slippers. Central Asian mantı (ravioli) and baklava desserts, no alcohol.

Ahırkapı
Map H7. Armada Hotel, Ahır Kapı Sok 24. Tel 0212 455 44 55. **Moderate**
A 1930s-style Turkish tavern with live fasil music performed by a female singer. Delicious meze and main dishes such as yoğurtlu yaprak dolması (minced meat in vine leaves with yogurt). Rooftop terrace with good views.

Rami
Map H6. Utangaç Sok 6. Tel 0212 517 65 93. **Moderate**
Owned by the son of Rami, an impressionist painter. Ottoman specialities include hünkar beğendi (meat in aubergine sauce). Views of Blue Mosque son-et-lumière from the terrace.

Valide Sultan Konagi
Map H6. Kutlugün Sok 1. Tel 0212 638 06 00. **Moderate**
Rooftop restaurant with stunning views of the sea and historic sights. Varied menu including mezes, doner and şiş kebabs, seafood and pizza.

CAFÉS

Lale Pudding Shop
Map G6. Divanyolu Cad 6.
A hippie hangout in the 1970s, it is now an inexpensive self-service cafeteria, serving casseroles, grilled chicken and milk puddings.

Rumeli
Map G6. Ticarethane Sok 8.
Chic designer café, created by an interior architect and decorated in stone and brick, featuring jazz, cabaret and classical music.

SHOPPING

Cavalry Bazaar
Map G7. Arasta Çarşisi, Sultanahmet Square.
Carpets are the main items, but handicrafts and jewellery are also on sale at these converted Ottoman stables.

Sofa
Map G6. Nuruosmaniye Cad 85. Cağaloğlu.
Sells antique and reproduction calligraphy as well as ebru (marbled paintings) and reproductions of Ottoman miniature paintings.

See p80 for price codes.

THE BAZAAR QUARTER

The importance of trade for Istanbul is evident in the warren of streets between the Galata Bridge and the Grand Bazaar. With its seemingly limitless range of goods, the bazaars are at the heart of all this activity. On the hill, next to the university, is the superb Süleymaniye Mosque.

SIGHTS AT A GLANCE

Mosques and Churches
Kalenderhane Mosque **7**
New Mosque **1**
Prince's Mosque **6**
Rüstem Paşa Mosque **3**
Süleymaniye Mosque **5** ✴
Tulip Mosque **8**

Bazaars, Hans and Shops
Book Bazaar **11** ✴
Grand Bazaar **13** ✴

Spice Bazaar **2**
Valide Hanı **12**

Museums and Monuments
Museum of Calligraphy **9**

Squares and Waterways
Beyazıt Square **10**
Golden Horn **4**

SEE ALSO

• *Street Life p41.*

KEY

⛴ Ferry boarding point
🚊 Tram stop
🚌 Main bus stop

| 0 metres | 600 |
| 0 yards | 600 |

◀ Brightly decorated candle lanterns in the Grand Bazaar

The New Mosque, a prominent feature on the Eminönü waterfront

New Mosque ❶

Map G4. Yeni Cami Meydanı, Eminönü. Open daily (except at prayer times). Free.

The New Mosque, at the southern end of Galata Bridge, testifies to the power of some women from the harem. Started in 1597 by Safiye, mother of Mehmet III, it was left unfinished when he died and she lost her position. Turhan Hadice, mother of Mehmet IV, completed it in 1663. In typical Ottoman style, the mosque has a vast courtyard, and once had a hospital, school and public baths. The tiled lunettes and bold Koranic frieze on the porch between courtyard and prayer hall are particularly striking.

Spice Bazaar ❷

Map F5. Cami Meydanı Sok. Open Mon–Sat. Free.

This cavernous, L-shaped market was built in the early 17th century as an extension of the New Mosque complex. From medieval times spices were a vital and expensive part of cooking. They became the market's main produce, benefitting from Istanbul's site on the trade route between the East, where most spices were grown, and Europe. Stalls in the bazaar stock spices, herbs and other foods such as honey, nuts, sweetmeats and *pastırma* (cured beef), and today also household goods, toys and clothes and exotic aphrodisiacs.

A selection of nuts and seeds for sale in the Spice Bazaar

Rüstem Paşa Mosque ❸

Map F4. Hasııcılar Cad, Eminönü.
Open daily. Free.

This mosque was built in
1561 by the great architect
Sinan for Rüstem Paşa, son-
in-law of and grand vizier
to Süleyman I. The corrupt
Rüstem had salted away vast
sums of money. It shows
in the mosque's superb tile
decorations – no other
mosque in the city can rival
it. The interior is covered in
İznik tiles of the very finest
quality. Some of the best
tiles are on the galleries, and
the prayer hall is a riot of
different patterns.

*Floral İznik tiles adorning the
interior of Rüstem Paşa Mosque*

Golden Horn ❹

Map F4.

Often described as the
world's greatest natural harbour, the Golden Horn is a
flooded river valley which
flows southwest into the
Bosphorus. The estuary
attracted settlers to its shores
in the 7th century BC and
later enabled Constantinople
to become a rich and powerful port. According to leg-
end, the Byzantines threw
so many valuables into the
waters during the Ottoman

conquest that the waters
glistened with gold. Today,
however, the Horn has
become polluted. For
centuries, merchants' ships
off-loaded their goods into
warehouses lining the
Golden Horn, but today the
great container ships use
ports on the Sea of Marmara
instead. Spanning the mouth
of the Horn is the Galata
Bridge (1992), which joins
Eminönü to Galata. It affords
great views of the cityscape.

Süleymaniye Mosque ❺

Map E5. Prof Sıddık Sami Onar
Caddesi, Vefa. Open daily (parts
closed for restoration until 2010).
Closed at prayer times. Free.

Istanbul's most important
mosque is both a tribute to
its architect, the great Sinan,
and a fitting memorial to its
founder, Süleyman the Magnificent. Built in 1550–57, it
was not only a place of wor-
ship, but also a charitable
foundation, or *külliye*. The
mosque is surrounded by
its former hospital, kitchen,
schools, caravanserai and
bath house, which fed and
cared for over 1,000 of the
city's poor – Muslims, Jews
and Christians alike.

Süleymaniye Mosque interior

Dome of the Prince's Mosque

Prince's Mosque ❻

Map D5. Şehzade Başı Cad 70, Saraçhane. Open daily. Tombs open for visitors Tue–Sun. Free.

This mosque complex was erected by Süleyman the Magnificent in memory of his eldest son by Roxelana, Şehzade (Prince) Mehmet, who died of smallpox at the age of 21. His tomb and those of grand viziers İbrahim Paşa and Rüstem Paşa, are the finest in the city. Each has beautiful İznik tiles and lustrous original stained glass. Sinan's first major imperial commission, he designed the mosque (1548) in a delightful decorative style that he later abandoned. You enter through an elegant porticoed inner courtyard, while the other institutions in the complex are enclosed in an outer courtyard. Unusually, the mosque is symmetrical, with a semi-dome on all four sides.

Kalenderhane Mosque ❼

Map E5. 16 Mart Şehitleri Cad, Saraçhane. Open at prayer times only. Free.

This Byzantine church was built and rebuilt several times between the 6th and 12th centuries, before being converted into a mosque shortly after the conquest in 1453. It is named after the Kalender brotherhood of dervishes. Just before conversion, it was the Church of Theotokos Kyriotissa (her Ladyship Mary, Mother of God). Some of the decoration survives in the prayer hall with its marble panelling, and in the fragments of fresco in the entrance hall.

A shaft of light illuminating the interior of Kalenderhane Mosque

The Baroque Tulip Mosque, housing a marketplace in its basement

Tulip Mosque ❽

Map D6. Ordu Cad, Laleli. Open at prayer times only. Free.

This Baroque mosque (1759–63) was built by Mehmet Tahir Ağa, who was best known for this style. The area under the main body, now an underground market, is a great hall on eight piers with a fountain.

Museum of Calligraphy

Museum of Calligraphy ❾

Map E6. Beyazıt Meydanı, Beyazıt. Open Tue–Sat. Adm charge.

The museum, in a delightful courtyard, takes its changing displays from the massive archives of the Turkish Calligraphy Foundation. Exhibits include fine manuscripts, calligraphy on stone and glass and calligraphers' tools.

Beyazıt Square ❿

Map E6. Ordu Cad, Beyazıt. Free.

Beyazıt Square is the most vibrant space in the old part of the city and the venue for a flea market throughout the week. Cafés invite for a rest in the shade. On the northern side of the square is the Moorish-style gateway into Istanbul University. The university's main building dates from the 19th century and once served as the Ministry of War. Beyazıt Mosque, the oldest surviving imperial mosque in the city, is on the square's eastern side.

The fortress-like entrance to Istanbul University, Beyazıt Square

Customers browsing in the charming Book Bazaar

Book Bazaar ⑪

Map F6. Sahaflar Çarşısı Sok, Beyazıt. Open daily. Free.

The booksellers' courtyard, on the site of the Byzantine book and paper market, has everything from tourist guides to academic tomes. In the centre stands the bust of İbrahim Müteferrika, who in 1729 printed the first book in the Turkish language, an Arabic dictionary.

Valide Hanı ⑫

Map F5. Junction of Çakmakçılar Yokuşu & Tarakçılar Cad, Beyazıt. Open Mon–Sat.

A huge area of commercial activity reaches all the way to the Golden Horn. Most manufacturing and trade takes place in *hans*, courtyards behind shaded gateways. The largest is Valide

Han, built in 1651. You enter it from Çakmakçılar Yokuşu through a massive portal. After an irregularly shaped forecourt, you come out into a large courtyard centring on a Shiite mosque. This was built when the han became the centre of Persian trade in the city. Today, it throbs to the rhythm of hundreds of weaving looms. A short walk further down Çakmakçılar Yokuşu is Büyük Yeni Han, a Baroque han built in 1764 on three arcaded levels.

Grand Bazaar ⑬

Map F6. Küçük Ayasofya Cad. Open daily.

Nothing can prepare you for the Grand Bazaar. This labyrinth of streets covered by painted vaults is lined with thousands of booth-like shops, whose wares spill out to tempt you and whose shopkeepers are relentless in their quest for a sale. The bazaar was established by Mehmet II shortly after his conquest of the city in 1453. It can be entered by several gateways, such as Çarşıkapı Gate and Nuruosmaniye Gate. It is easy to get lost in the bazaar in spite of the signposting.

Rugs on display at the Grand Bazaar

STREET LIFE

RESTAURANTS

Havuzlu
Map F6. Gani Çelebi Sok 3, Grand Bazaar, Beyazıt. Tel 0212 527 33 46. **Cheap**
A simple, authentic restaurant that serves soups, dolmas, şiş kebab and grilled meats.

Borsa
Map G5. Yalı Köşkü Cad 60, Sirkeci. Tel 0212 527 23 50. **Cheap**
Traditional restaurant with a varied menu, including Turkish dishes such as beğendili kebab (meat in aubergine sauce). There is also a self-service section for quick lunches.

Darüzziyafe
Map E4. Şifahane Cad 6, Beyazıt. Tel 0212 511 84 14. **Cheap**
Stunning restaurant in the former kitchens of the Süley-manye Mosque. Ottoman-inspired food. No alcohol.

Karaca
Map F/G6. Gazi Sinan Paşa Sok 1/A, Cağaloğlu. Tel 0212 512 90 94. **Cheap**
Large restaurant, popular with shopkeepers, in a former caravanserai. Turkish food including pazı dolması (stuffed chard leaves with yoghurt) and islim kebabı (lamb with aubergine) plus fish in winter.

Subaşı
Map F/G6. Nuruosmaniye Cad 48, Çarşıkapı. Tel 0212 522 47 62. **Cheap**
Simple restaurant on two floors offering basic Turkish fare. A convenient lunch stop near the Grand Bazaar.

Pandeli
Map F4. Mısır Çarşısı 1, Eminönü. Tel 0212 527 39 09. **Moderate**
Istanbul's oldest restaurant, situated in the Spice Bazaar. Famous for kağıtta levrek (sea bass cooked in wax paper) and kılıç şiş (swordfish kebab).

Orient House
Map F6. Tiyatro Cad 27, Çarşıkapı. Tel 0212 517 61 63. **Expensive**
A cultural evening offers dinner, Turkish music and belly dancing. Booking required.

SHOPPING

Galeri Şirvan
Map F6. Keseciler Cad 55–7, Grand Bazaar.
Carpet shop specializing in Anatolian tribal kelims.

Muhlis Günbattı
Map F6. Perdahçılar Paşa Sok 48, Grand Bazaar.
Rare Central Asian textiles, Uzbek and Turkmen hand-appliquéd cloths, silk ikats and Ottoman kaftans and carpets.

Sivaslı Yazmacısı
Map F6. Yağlıkçılar Sok 57, Grand Bazaar.
Fabric shop, selling village tex-tiles, crocheted headscarves and embroidered cloths.

May
Map F6. Koltuik Kazazlar Sok 10, Grand Bazaar.
One of the best pottery shops in the Bazaar, selling a large range of plates, bowls, Turkish coffee cups and vases.

See p80 for price codes.

BEYOĞLU

For centuries Beyoğlu, a steep hill north of the Golden Horn, was home to the city's foreign residents who came to trade. The district, dominated by the Galata Tower, has not changed much in character over the centuries and is still a thriving commercial quarter today.

SIGHTS AT A GLANCE

Historic Buildings and Monuments

Galata Tower **4**
Mevlevi Monastery **3**
Pera Palas Hotel **1**

Mosques and Churches

Church of SS Peter and Paul **5**
Kılıç Ali Paşa Mosque **7**
Yeraltı Mosque **6**

Streets and Quarters

Çukurcuma **8**
İstiklal Caddesi **2**
Taksim **9**

SEE ALSO

• Street Life p47.

KEY

⚓	Ferry boarding point
🚊	Tram stop
🚌	Main bus stop
🚋	Nostalgic tram stop
Ⓜ	Metro station
🚟	Funicular (Tünel) stop
ℹ	Tourist information office

0 metres   800

0 yards   800

◀ The Galata Tower and backstreets of Beyoğlu

Exterior of the Pera Palas Hotel circa 1929

Pera Palas Hotel ❶

Map G2. Meşrutiyet Cad 98–100, Tepebaşı. Closed for restoration until late 2009.

The evocative Pera Palas has changed little since it opened in 1892, to cater for travellers on the Orient Express. The Grand Orient bar serves cocktails beneath its original chandeliers, while the patisserie offers irresistible cakes and a genteel ambience. Among its former legendary guests were Agatha Christie, Mata Hari, Atatürk and Jackie Onassis.

İstiklal Caddesi ❷

Map G 1/2. Meşrutiyet Cad 98–100, Tepebaşı.

This pedestrianized street, once known as Grande Rue de Pera, is lined by late 19th-century apartment blocks and European consulates. In the backstreets are churches serving the foreign communities as well as trendy jazz clubs, craft shops, stylish restaurants and the lively Galatasaray Fish Market.

Mevlevi Monastery ❸

Map G2. Galip Dede Cad 15, Beyoğlu. Open Wed–Mon. Adm charge.

The monastery belonged to the most famous Sufi sect, the Whirling Dervishes. When Sufism was banned by Atatürk in 1924, it became a museum, with the sect's clothing, manuscripts, photographs and musical instruments on display. On the last Sunday of every month at 3pm, the *sema*, a ritual dance, is performed by latter-day Sufis on a beautiful wooden dance floor.

A performance of the Whirling Dervishes at the Mevlevi Monastery

Galata Tower ❹

Map G3. Büyük Hendek Sok, Beyoğlu. Open daily. Restaurant & Nightclub open daily. Adm charge.

The most recognizable feature on the Golden Horn, the Galata Tower, is 62 m (205 ft) high and topped by a conical tower. It was built in 1384 by the Genoese as part of their fortifications. After the conquest of Istanbul in 1453, the Ottomans turned it into a prison and naval depot. In the 17th century, aviation pioneer, Hezarfen Ahmet Çelebi, attached

Door in the Church of SS Peter and Paul

wings to his arms and "flew" from the tower to Üsküdar. The building was subsequently used as a fire watchtower. The tower has been renovated and on the ninth floor there is now a restaurant and nightclub. The unmissable view from the balcony encompasses the main monuments on the Istanbul skyline and beyond.

The Galata Tower, dominating the skyline in Beyoğlu

Church of SS Peter and Paul ❺

Map G3. Galata Kulesi Sok 44, Karaköy. Open daily. Ring the bell to gain admittance. Free.

Their original church was requisitioned as a mosque in the early 1500s, and so the Dominicans of Galata moved to this site, just below the Tower. The present building, dating from 1841, was built by the Fossati brothers. The rear wall is built into a section of the old Genoese ramparts. According to Ottoman rules, the main façade of the church could not be on a road so it is reached through a tiny door and courtyard. A basilica in style, it has four side altars and a sky-blue cupola, studded with gold stars.

Yeraltı Mosque ❻

Map G3. Karantina Sok, Karaköy. Open daily. Free.

This mosque, literally "the underground mosque", contains the shrines of two Muslim saints, Abu Sufyan and Amiri Wahibi, who died during the first Arab siege of the city in the 7th century. It was the discovery of their bodies in the cellar of an ancient Byzantine fortification in 1640 that led to the creation of first a shrine on the site and later, in 1757, a mosque. The tombs are at the end of a low, dark prayer hall, whose roof is supported by pillars.

Koranic inscription in İznik tiles at the Kılıç Ali Paşa Mosque

Kılıç Ali Paşa Mosque ⑦

Map H3. Necatibey Cad, Tophane. Open daily. Free.

This mosque, built in 1580 by Sinan, was inspired by Haghia Sophia. İznik tiles adorn the mihrab and there is a delightful deep porch before the main door. Kılıç Ali Paşa, who commissioned the mosque, was captured by Muslim pirates and later converted to Islam under Süleyman the Magnificent (1520–66). He served as a naval commander under three sultans. After retiring he asked Murat III where to build his mosque. The sultan replied "in the admiral's domain, the sea", and Kılıç Ali Paşa took him at his word, reclaiming part of the Bosphorus for his complex.

Monument of Independence, Taksim

Çukurcuma ⑧

Map H2.

This charming old quarter of Beyoğlu has become an important centre for the furnishings and antiques trades. Converted warehouses have modern upholstery materials piled up in carved marble basins and antique cabinets. A place for bargain-hunting.

Taksim ⑨

Map H1.

The Taksim area, around Taksim Square, is the hub of activity in modern Beyoğlu. Taksim means "water distribution centre", and from the early 18th century it was from this site that water from the Belgrade Forest was distributed throughout the city. The original stone reservoir, built in 1732 by Mahmut I, still stands at the top of İstiklâl Caddesi. In the southwest of the square is the 1928 Monument of Independence, by Canonica. It shows Atatürk and the other founding fathers of the Turkish Republic. Further up, on Cumhuriyet Caddesi, is the Taksim Art Gallery. As well as temporary exhibitions, the gallery has a permanent display of cityscapes by 20th-century painters.

STREET LIFE

RESTAURANTS

Lades
Map H1. Sadri Alisik Sok 14, Beyoğlu. Tel 0212 251 32 03. **Cheap**
Attractive little lokanta, serving simple, tasty home-style food in a cosy atmosphere. Few meat dishes, but try the lahana dolması. No alcohol.

Nature and Peace
Map H1. Büyükparmakkapı Sok 21, Beyoğlu. Tel 0212 252 86 09. **Cheap**
One of the best health food restaurants, offering a selection of vegetable, chicken and fish dishes but no red meat. Great pastries and fruit juices.

Yakup 2
Map G2. Asmalı Mescit Cad 21, Tünel. Tel 0212 249 29 25. **Cheap**
A friendly, connoisseur's eating and drinking spot, serving a memorable selection of mezes and fish dishes.

Galata House
Map G3. Galata Kulesi Sok 15. Tel 0212 245 18 61. **Moderate**
This is a true original – a restaurant in a converted British jail, with prisoners' graffiti amid the bric-a-brac. It serves a delicious Russian-Georgian-Turkish menu.

Changa
Map H1. Sıraselviler Cad 47. Tel 0212 249 13 48. **Expensive**
This stylish modern restaurant in an Art-Nouveau building serves fabulous Pacific-fusion cuisine. An inset glass floor allows guests to watch the chefs below.

Panorama
Map H1. Marmara Hotel, Taksim Square. Tel 0212 251 46 96. **Expensive**
This elegant restaurant at the top of the high-rise hotel affords stunning views of the Bosphorus, the Golden Horn and Sea of Marmara. Gourmet Turkish, French and Italian food, rich Ottoman-inspired décor, weekend jazz.

CAFÉS AND PATISSERIES

Culina Café
Map G1. Akarsu Sok (off Yeni Çarşı Cad).
An intimate corner café with vintage-style cushions and other kitsch. Also serves meals.

İnci Patisserie
Map H1. İstiklal Cad 156.
Famous for its excellent profiteroles and baklava, run-down looking but always busy.

SHOPPING

Aznavur Pasaji
Map G1. İstiklal Cad 212.
Hand-made crafts in silver, ceramic and marble.

Koton
Map G1. İstiklal Cad 54.
Men's and women's fashion at this reasonably priced Turkish chain store.

Paşabahçe
Map G2. İstiklal Cad 150.
The largest glass manufacturer in Turkey. Creates delicate çeşmibülbül vases (decorated with blue and gold stripes) and Beykoz-style ware (with gilded decoration).

See p80 for price codes.

Fishing boats in one of the attractive ports on the Bosphorus ▶

GREATER ISTANBUL

Many sights in Greater Istanbul are also worth exploring. It has been divided into five areas (see below); each also has its own map. Closest to the centre are the mosques and churches of Fatih, Fener and Balat: most conspicuously the gigantic Fatih Mosque. Across the Golden Horn from Balat the Aynalı Kavak Palace is worth visiting. The Theodosian Walls, stretching from the Golden Horn to the Sea of Marmara, are one of the city's most impressive monuments. Along these walls stands the Church of St Saviour in Chora, with its stunning Byzantine mosaics. Beyond the walls, up the Golden Horn, is Eyüp, a focus of pilgrimage to Muslims, where you can visit a number of fine mausoleums. Following the Bosphorus northwards past Beyoğlu brings you to the Dolmabahçe Palace, an opulent fantasy created in the 19th century by Sultan Abdül Mecit I. The Asian side has a handsome railway station and a Florence Nightingale museum.

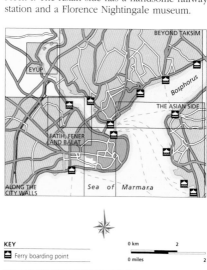

KEY

🛳 Ferry boarding point

0 km	2
0 miles	2

◀ Fountain in the grounds of the sumptuous Dolmabahçe Palace

Fatih, Fener and Balat

For centuries after the Muslim conquest, a large number of Jews and Christians lived in Istanbul. Balat was home to Greek-speaking Jews from the Byzantine era onwards, who were later joined by Sephardic Jews from Spain. Fener became a Greek enclave in the early 1500s; many of its residents rose to prominent positions in the Ottoman Empire. Fatih is linked to the city's radical Islamic tradition.

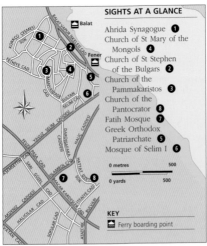

SIGHTS AT A GLANCE

Ahrida Synagogue **1**
Church of St Mary of the Mongols **4**
Church of St Stephen of the Bulgars **2**
Church of the Pammakaristos **3**
Church of the Pantocrator **8**
Fatih Mosque **7**
Greek Orthodox Patriarchate **5**
Mosque of Selim I **6**

| 0 metres | | 500 |
| 0 yards | | 500 |

KEY

 Ferry boarding point

Ahrida Synagogue **1**

Gevgili Sok, Balat. Open only for guided tours and by prior arrangement. Free.

Istanbul's oldest synagogue, founded before the Muslim conquest of the city in 1453, has beautifully restored painted Baroque walls and ceilings. Pride of place, however, goes to the central Holy Ark, covered in rich tapestries, which contains rare holy scrolls.

Church of St Stephen of the Bulgars **2**

Mürsel Paşa Cad 85, Balat. Open daily. Free.

This entire church was cast in iron in Vienna in 1871, shipped to the Golden Horn and assembled on its shore. It was needed and is still used by the Bulgarian community who had broken away from the authority of the Greek Orthodox Patriarchate just up the hill.

Church of the Pammakaristos **3**

Fethiye Cad, Draman. Open at prayer times only. Adm charge.

One of Istanbul's hidden secrets, this church housed the Greek Orthodox Patriarchate, but was converted into a mosque in the late 16th century. The charming exterior is Byzantine, with its alternating stone and brick courses and carved marble details. The main building is the working mosque, while the stunning mosaics are in a side chapel. You need permission from Haghia Sophia to visit this museum, but the caretaker may let you in. The 14th-century mosaics show holy figures in a sea of gold, a reflection of the heavens. In the centre of the main dome stand Christ Pantocrator ("the All-Powerful") and the Old Testament prophets. In the apse Christ is seated on a jewel-encrusted throne, the Virgin Mary and John the Baptist at his sides, overlooked by the four archangels.

Detail on the Church of St Mary of the Mongols

Church of St Mary of the Mongols **4**

Tevkii Cafer Mektebi Sok, Fener. Open by appointment. Free.

Consecrated in the late 13th century, this church was decreed immune from conversion to a mosque and has been in the hands of the Greek community since the Byzantine era. A copy of the decree is kept by the church. It is named after its founder, Maria Palaeologina, an illegitimate Byzantine princess who lived with her Mongol husband in Persia. On his assassination, she returned to build this church. A beautiful Byzantine mosaic which depicts Theotokos Pammakaristos ("the All-Joyous Mother of God") is the church's greatest treasure.

Byzantine façade of the Church of the Pammakaristos

Interior of the Church of St George in the Greek Orthodox Patriarchate

Greek Orthodox Patriarchate ❺

Sadrazam Ali Paşa Cad 35, Fener. Open daily. Guided tours. Free.

This walled complex has been the seat of the patriarch of the Greek Orthodox Church since the early 17th century. Though nominally head of the whole church, the patriarch is now shepherd to a diminishing flock in and around Istanbul.

The main door of the Patriarchate has been welded shut in memory of Patriarch Gregory V, who was hanged here for treason in 1821 after encouraging the Greeks to overthrow Ottoman rule at the start of the Greek War of Independence (1821–32).

The Patriarchate centres on the basilica-style Church of St George which dates back to 1720. Yet the church contains much older relics and furniture. The patriarch's throne, the high structure to the right of the nave, is thought to be Byzantine, while the pulpit on the left is adorned with fine wooden inlay and Orthodox icons.

Mosque of Selim I ❻

Yavuz Selim Cad, Fener. Open daily. Free.

This much-admired mosque (1522) has an air of neglect, yet its intimate courtyard gives an insight into the concept of paradise in Islam. At the centre of this lovely garden is an octagonal, domed fountain, surrounded by trees. The portico windows are capped by early İznik tiles. The simple prayer hall has fine mosque furniture.

İznik tile panel capping a window in the Mosque of Selim I

Chandelier hanging in the light and airy interior of Fatih Mosque

Fatih Mosque ❼

Macar Kardeşler Cad, Fatih. Open daily. Free.

A spacious courtyard surrounds this vast Baroque edifice (1771), built on the site of earlier mosques, the first of which collapsed in an earthquake in 1766. İznik tiles and lunettes with calligraphic marble inlay adorn the windows in the original porticoes. You can admire the tomb of Mehmet the Conqueror, with an appropriately large sarcophagus and turban, and of his consort Gülbahar. It is a place of enormous gravity, always busy with supplicants.

Church of the Pantocrator ❽

İbadethane Sok, Küçükpazar. Open daily at prayer times. Free.

The church was once the centrepiece of a monastery complex including a church, a hospice for the elderly, an asylum and a hospital. Now it is a mosque, composed of three chapels. The highest was built by Empress Irene, founder of the Church of the Pantocrator ("Christ the Almighty") in the 12th century, with additions made by Emperor John II after her death in 1124. The interior boasts a magnificent figurative marble floor.

Church of the Pantocrator, built in the 12th century

STREET LIFE

RESTAURANTS	SHOPPING
Sedef	**Wednesday Street Market**
Fevzi Paşa Cad 19, Fatih.	Fatih Mosque.
Tel 0212 532 82 33.	*This weekly market turns the*
Moderate	*streets around the mosque*
This is a bright and spacious	*into a circus of commerce.*
restaurant that prides itself on	*From tables piled high with*
its meat dishes. Grilled meats	*fruit and vegetables to lorries*
are the most popular, but do	*loaded with unspun wool, this*
not overlook the delicious	*is a real spectacle.*
vegetable stews. Alcohol is	
not served.	See p80 for price codes.

Along the City Walls

Istanbul's land walls are one of the most impressive remains of the city's Byzantine past. Pierced by monumental gates and strengthened by towers, they surround the city centre in a great arc, stretching from Yedikule on the Sea of Marmara to Ayvansaray on the Golden Horn. The suburbs that lie adjacent to the walls are mainly residential districts, interspersed with wasteland that it is unsafe to explore alone. Dotted around these suburbs, however, are important sights, including the outstanding Church of St Saviour in Chora.

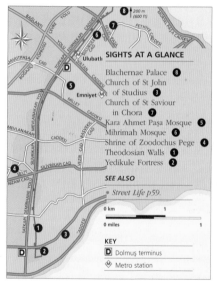

SIGHTS AT A GLANCE

Blachernae Palace   **8**
Church of St John
of Studius   **3**
Church of St Saviour
in Chora   **7**
Kara Ahmet Paşa Mosque   **5**
Mihrimah Mosque   **6**
Shrine of Zoodochus Pege   **4**
Theodosian Walls   **1**
Yedikule Fortress   **2**

SEE ALSO

0 km		1

0 miles		1

KEY

D   Dolmuş terminus

Ⓜ   Metro station

Theodosian Walls ❶

From Yedikule to Ayvansaray.
Open daily. Free.

Built during the reign of Theodosius II in AD 412–22, this great chain of double walls extends for 6.5 km (4 miles). With its 11 fortified gates and 192 towers, it protected the city from landward invasion for more than a thousand years. In 447 an earthquake destroyed 54 of the towers; they were rebuilt to keep out Attila the Hun.

Silivrikapı, one of the gateways through the Theodosian Walls

Subsequently they resisted sieges by Arabs, Bulgarians, Russians and Turks. The armies of the Fourth Crusade stormed the ramparts along the Golden Horn, and Mehmet the Conqueror finally breached the walls in 1453. They fell into disrepair in the late 17th century, but large stretches have now been rebuilt and give an idea of how the walls used to look. Many of the gateways are still in good repair.

Yedikule Fortress ❷

Yedikule Meydanı Sok, Yedikule. Open Thu–Tue. Adm charge.

Yedikule, the "Fortress of the Seven Towers", is a five-sided fortification on the southern section of the Theodosian Walls. The fortress today has both Byzantine and Ottoman features. The tower to the left as you enter is "the tower with inscriptions". A prison for foreign envoys and those who fell foul of the sultan, it bears its inmates' carvings.

Church of St John of Studius ❸

Imam Aşir Sok, Yedikule. Free.

Istanbul's oldest surviving church, St John of Studius, is now a mere shell, consisting only of the outer walls. Built in AD 463 by Studius, a Roman patrician, it became a spiritual and intellectual centre in the late 8th century, under the rule of Abbot Theodore, who was buried in the church's garden. Until its removal by Crusaders, the most sacred relic housed in the church was the head of St John the Baptist.

Shrine of Zoodochus Pege ❹

Seyit Nizam Cad 3, Silivrikapı. Open daily. Free.

The Fountain of the "Life-Giving Spring" is built over a sacred and miraculous spring. The fish here are supposed to have leapt into it from a monk's frying pan on hearing him declare that a Turkish invasion of Constantinople was as likely as fish coming back to life.

The Shrine of Zoodochus Pege

Tilework over medrese doorway at Kara Ahmet Paşa Mosque

Kara Ahmet Paşa Mosque **5**

Undeğirmeni Sok, Fatma Sultan.
Open prayer times only. Free.

This lovely and gracefully
proportioned mosque was
built by Sinan in 1554 for
Kara Ahmet Paşa. Its peaceful leafy courtyard is surrounded by the cells of a
medrese and a *dershane*, or
main classroom. Attractive
apple-green and yellow
16th-century İznik tiles adorn
the porch and the east wall
of the prayer hall.

Window in the Mihrimah Mosque

Mihrimah Mosque **6**

Sulukule Cad, Edirnekapı. Open
daily. Free.

An imposing monument
located just inside the city
walls, the Mihrimah Mosque
complex was built by Sinan
in 1562–5. Mihrimah was the
daughter of Süleyman the
Magnificent. The mosque
rests on a platform, and
occupying the highest point
in the city, it is visible from
afar on the Bosphorus.

The square building has
four strong turrets at its
corners, and is surmounted
by a 37-m (121-ft) high
dome. The single minaret is
tall and slender, so much so
that it has been destroyed by
earthquakes twice. On the
second occasion, in 1894,
the minaret crashed through
the roof of the mosque. The
20th-century stencilling on
the inside of the prayer hall
was added after this incident.

The interior is illuminated
by numerous windows,
some of which have stained
glass. The supporting arches
of the sultan's loge have
been skilfully painted to
resemble green-and-white
marble. The carved marbled
minbar is also impressive.

Church of St Saviour in Chora **7**

Kariye Camii Sok, Kariye Meydanı, Edirnekapı. Open daily. Adm charge.

Some of the very finest Byzantine mosaics and frescoes can be found in this church. Little is known of its early history. The present church dates from the 11th century. It was remodelled in 1315–21 and the mosaics and frescoes were added by Theodore Metochites, an eminent intellectual and official of his day.

The four main cycles of mosaics represent: *The Genealogy of Christ*, in the inner narthex, portraying 66 of Christ's forebears; the *Life*

View of the domes and semidomes of St Saviour in Chora

of the Virgin, based mainly on the 2nd-century Gospel of St James; *The Infancy of Christ*, on the panels of the outer narthex, based largely on the New Testament; and *Christ's Ministry*, in the vaults of the outer narthex.

The church also has beautiful frescoes in the parecclesion, painted around 1320. The most fascinating of these is the *Anastasis* in a semidome above the apse.

Blachernae Palace **8**

Ivaz Ağa Cad, Ayvansaray. Adm charge.

The scant remains of this palace consist of a tower in the city wall, known as the Prison of Anemas, a terrace to the east (the present site of a mosque), and the Tower of Isaac Angelus. The Anemas tower has fragments of the marble decoration and wall frescoes. Dating back to AD 500, the palace was an occasional residence for imperial visitors to the shrine of Blachernae. The great Comnenus emperors rebuilt the structure in the 12th century, transforming it into a magnificent palace.

STREET LIFE

RESTAURANTS

Develi

Gümüşyüzük Sok 7, Samatya Balik Pazan, Kocamustafapaşa. Tel 0212 632 79 82.
Cheap
Serves spicy meat specialities from southeastern Anatolia. Try kebabı malta erik (with pistachios and loquat), keme (with mushrooms) or patlıcan (with aubergine).

Asitane

Kariye Hotel, Kariye camii Sok 18, Edirnekapı. Tel 0212 534 84. *Moderate*
Ottoman fare in the atmospheric hotel dining room or on the terrace. Try the desserts: kadırga pilavı (rice with almonds and pistachios) and incir tatlısı (figs with walnuts).

See p80 for price codes.

Eyüp

As the burial place of Eyüp Ensari, the standard bearer of the Prophet Mohammed, the tranquil village of Eyüp is a sacrosanct place of pilgrimage for Muslims from all over the world. The wealthy elite established mosques and street fountains in the village but, above all, they chose Eyüp as a place of burial. Their grand mausoleums line the streets surrounding Eyüp Sultan Mosque.

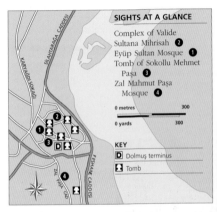

SIGHTS AT A GLANCE

Complex of Valide
Sultana Mihrisah ❷
Eyüp Sultan Mosque ❶
Tomb of Sokollu Mehmet
Paşa ❸
Zal Mahmut Paşa
Mosque ❹

| 0 metres | 300 |
| 0 yards | 300 |

KEY

D Dolmuş terminus

🛈 Tomb

Eyüp Sultan Mosque ❶

Cami-i Kebir Cad. Open daily.
Free.

Mehmet the Conqueror built the original mosque on this site in 1458, in honour of Eyüp Ensari. The present mosque, by Selim III, dates from 1800. The delightful inner courtyard is planted with two huge plane trees on a platform. This was the setting for the Girding of the Sword of Osman, part of a sultan's inauguration ceremony. The mosque itself is predominantly covered in gleaming white marble.

Complex of Valide Sultana Mihrişah ❷

Seyit Reşat Cad. Open Tue–Sun.
Free.

Most of the northern side of the street leading from Eyüp Mosque's northern gate is occupied by the largest Baroque *külliye* in Istanbul, although unusually it is not centred on a mosque. Built in 1791 for Mihrişah, mother of Selim III, the complex includes the ornate marble tomb of Mihrişah and a soup kitchen, which is still in use today. There is also a beautiful grilled fountain.

Tomb of Sokollu Mehmet Paşa ❸

Cami-i Kebir Cad. Open Tue–Sun. Free.

Grand vizier Sokollu Mehmet Paşa commissioned his tomb around 1574, five years before he was assassinated by a madman in the Topkapı Palace. The famous architect Sinan built this elegantly proportioned eight-sided tomb. It is notable for its stained glass, some of which is original. A roofed colonnade connects the tomb to what was formerly a Koranic school.

Zal Mahmut Paşa Mosque

Zal Mahmut Paşa Mosque ❹

Zal Paşa Cad. Open daily. Free.

Heading south from the centre of Eyüp, it is a short walk to Zal Mahmut Paşa Mosque. The complex was built by the great architect Sinan for the man who assassinated Mustafa, the first-born heir of Süleyman the Magnificent. Probably erected some time in the 1560s, the mosque is notable for the lovely floral tiles around its *mihrab*, and for its carved marble *minbar* and *müezzin mahfili*. Down some steps to the north of the mosque is the garden. Here stands the large tomb of Zal Mahmut Paşa and his wife, said to have both died on the same day. On the same street, Cezri Kasım Paşa Mosque (1515) is a small mosque with a pretty portal and a tiled *mihrab*.

Visitors at the tomb of Eyüp Ensari, opposite Eyüp Sultan Mosque

STREET LIFE

CAFÉS

Pierre Loti Café

Gümüşsuyu Karyağdı Sok 5, Eyüp.

This famous *kahve* stands at the top of the hill in Eyüp cemetery, from where it commands sweeping views of the Golden Horn. It is named after the French novelist and Turkophile who is said to have frequented it in 1876. Loti, a French naval officer, was in love with a married Turkish woman and wrote an autobiographical novel, Aziyade. The café is decorated in tiles and has beautiful 19th-century furniture, the waiters wear period clothing. On the way to the café you will pass a picturesque array of Ottoman tombstones, including those of the executioners.

Beyond Taksim

The area to the North of Taksim Square became fashionable in the 19th century, when sultans built palaces along the Bosphorus and in the wooded hills above. The extravagant Dolmabahçe Palace, built by Abdül Mecit I, started the trend. High-ranking court officials soon followed, and the area achieved a glamour that it retains to this day. Among the sights worth seeing are the Aynalı Kavak Palace, the last surviving trace of a grand palace built by Ahmet III, and two museums, the Naval Museum and the impressive Military Museum.

SIGHTS AT A GLANCE

Aynalı Kavak Palace **8**

Dolmabahçe Palace and Mosque **6**

Military Museum **7**

Museum of Fine Arts **5**

Naval Museum **4**

Ortaköy **1**

Pavilion of the Linden Tree **3**

Yıldız Park **2**

KEY

🚢 Ferry boarding point

D Dolmuş terminus

🚠 Cable car station

0 km ——— 1

0 miles ——— 1

SEE ALSO

• Street Life p65

Ortaköy **1**

Ortaköy.

This suburb, at the foot of the Bosphorus Bridge, still has the feel of the fishing village it once was. Today, though, it is best known for its shops selling local artisans' products, its busy Sunday market in İskele Meydanı Square and its lively bar and café scene, especially in summer.

Yıldız Park **2**

Çırağan Cad, Beşiktaş. Open Tue–Sun. Yıldız Palace open Tue–Sun. Adm charge.

Yıldız Park surrounds Yıldız Palace, an assortment of 19th-and 20th-century pavilions and villas. The State Apartments are not open to the public. There are various museums – the City Museum shows Yıldız porcelain, the

The former armoury of Yıldız Palace, in Yıldız Park

Yıldız Palace Museum displays art and objects from the palace. There is also a museum in the Yıldız Palace Theatre. The most impressive building is the Şale Pavilion, built in three parts in the late 1800s, the last two for Kaiser Wilhelm II. Both Churchill and de Gaulle stayed in the oldest section. Worth seeing are the Mother-of-Pearl Salon and the beautiful Hereke carpet. Further pavilions and the former Imperial Porcelain Factory dot Yıldız Park. The park contains many ancient trees and exotic shrubs. It is sited on a steep hill – take a taxi to the Şale Pavilion and walk back down.

Pavilion of the Linden Tree ❸

Ihlamur Teşvikiye Yolu, Beşiktaş. **Open** Tue–Wed & Fri–Sun. Guided tours. Adm charge.

Once a grove of lime (linden) trees – hence the name – these beautiful, leafy gardens with magnolias, camellias and fountains once housed an early 19th-century sultans' residence. Abdül

Rowing boat used by Atatürk

Mecit chose Nikogos Balyan to design a new home here in 1857. Two pavilions were built, the grander of which is the Ceremonial Pavilion, or Mabeyn Köşkü, used by the sultan and his guests. The Entourage Pavilion, or Maiyet Köşkü, was reserved for the sultan's retinue. The façades are Baroque, with double stairways and decorative elements. The ornate interiors reflect 19th-century Ottoman and European styles.

Naval Museum ❹

Hayrettin Paşa İskelesi Sok, Beşiktaş. **Open** Wed–Sun. Guided tours. Adm charge.

This museum is undergoing major renovations and will be closed until 2008. One building, the Caïques Gallery, displays huge imperial rowing boats, or *caïques*, dating from the 17th century. The largest of these, at 40 m (130 ft), was used by Mehmet IV and powered by 144 oarsmen. The rowing boats used by Atatürk look tiny in comparison, yet he entertained heads of state in them.

Museum of Fine Arts ❺

Hayrettin Paşa İskelesi Sok,
Beşiktaş. Open Wed–Sat. Free.

The museum houses a fine
collection of 19th- and 20th-
century paintings and sculp-
ture. Westernization in the
19th century led artists like
Osman Hamdi Bey (1842–
1910) to experiment with
European art forms. Their
subject matter, however,
gives a glimpse into the
Oriental history of the city.

*Woman with Mimosas by Osman
Hamdi Bey, Museum of Fine Arts*

Dolmabahçe Palace and Mosque ❻

Dolmabahçe Cad, Edirnekapı.
Open Fri–Wed. Closed first day of
religious festivals. Guided tours
only. Adm charge. Mosque open
daily. Free.

Sultan Abdül Mecit built
Dolmabahçe Palace in 1856,
designed by Karabet and
Nikogos Balyan, Armenian
architects who created many
villas along the Bosphorus.
Extravagantly opulent, the
Dolmabahçe was actually
built when the Ottoman
Empire was in decline. The
sultan financed his great
palace with loans from foreign
banks. Guided tours lead
through the Selamlık (or
Mabeyn-i Hümayun), the part
of the palace reserved for men
and containing the state rooms

*Imperial Gate, the main entrance
to Dolmabahçe Palace*

and the Ceremonial Hall. The
other tour goes through the
Harem, the living quarters of
the sultan and his entourage.

One of the palace's star
features is the Crystal
Staircase, shaped like a
double horsehoe and made
from Baccarat crystal and
brass. The Süfera Salon,
where ambassadors awaited
their audience with the
sultan, is one of the most
luxurious rooms. The
Ceremonial Hall holds 2,500
guests. It has an English
chandelier, reputedly the
heaviest in the world.
Atatürk died in one of the
bedrooms; all palace clocks
display the time of his death.
The walls of the Main
Bathroom are held in finest
Egyptian alabaster and the
taps are solid silver.

The adjacent Dolmabahçe
Mosque (1853) was built by
the Garabe and Balyan
families. Its slim minarets are
shaped like Corinthian
columns, while great arching
windows lighten the interior.
Inside, the decoration
includes fake marbling and
trompe l'oeil painting.

Military Museum

Vali Konağı Cad, Harbiye.
Open Wed–Sun. Mehter Band
performances 3pm daily.
Guided tours. Adm charge.

The Military Museum traces the history of Turkey's conflicts from the 1453 conquest of Constantinople through to modern warfare. Among the most striking weapons on display are the 15th-century curved daggers (*cembiyes*) carried by foot soldiers. Other exhibits include the classroom where Atatürk studied in 1899–1905, head armour for horses, Ottoman cane-and-willow shields covered in silk, and spectacular embroidered silk tents used by the sultans on their campaigns. The Mehter Band also performs here. Thought to have inspired Beethoven and Mozart, the band accompanied the sultans into battle from the 14th century until the 19th century.

Ottoman daggers

Audience Chamber of Aynalı Kavak Palace on the Golden Horn

Aynalı Kavak Palace

Kasımpaşa Cad, Hasköy. Open
Tue, Wed, Fri–Sun. Adm charge.

The palace is the last vestige of an earlier large complex in extensive gardens on the Golden Horn. An inscription dated 1791 can be found all over, but it is likely to have been built earlier, by Ahmet III (1703–30). Sited on a hill, it has two storeys on one side and one on the other.

Original features include stained-glass windows, set in stucco tracery. Particularly striking is the Composition Room, which Sultan Selim III (1789–1807) is thought to have used for writing music.

STREET LIFE

RESTAURANTS

Ortaköy Manti Evi
Değirmen Sok 3/A, Ortaköy. Tel
0212 261 78 67. **Cheap**
Specializing in traditional dishes such as its namesake, manti, a Turkish dumpling served with yoghurt.

Hacıbey
Teşvikiye Cad 8/B, Teşvikiye. Tel
0212 231 71 34. **Cheap**

Modern and stylish, but still cooking on charcoal. Try Bursa kebabs, red lentil soup and kemalpaşa, a semolina dessert.

SHOPPING

Sunday Market, Ortaköy
İskele Meydanı Square.
Arts and crafts stalls crowd the waterfront square.

See p80 for price codes.

The Asian Side

The Asian side of Istanbul comprises the two major suburbs of Üsküdar and Kadıköy, which date from the 7th century BC. Üsküdar was the starting point of Byzantine trade routes through Asia. It retained its importance in the Ottoman period and today is renowned for its many classical mosques. A number of residential districts radiate from Üsküdar and Kadıköy. Prominent landmarks on this side of the Bosphorus are Leander's Tower and the Selimiye Barracks, made famous by Florence Nightingale. Haydarpaşa Station marked the advance of the railway across Anatolia and into Asia.

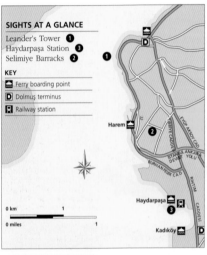

SIGHTS AT A GLANCE

Leander's Tower **1**
Haydarpaşa Station **3**
Selimiye Barracks **2**

KEY

⬛ Ferry boarding point

D Dolmuş terminus

🚉 Railway station

0 km | 1

0 miles | 1

Leander's tower, on a small island

Leander's Tower **1**

Üsküdar. Free.

The tiny, white Leander's Tower stands on its own islet, on the former site of a 12th-century Byzantine fortress. The 18th-century tower has served variously as a quarantine centre during a cholera outbreak, a lighthouse, a customs control point and a maritime toll gate. Today shipping is monitored from here. In Turkish, the tower is known as the "Maiden's Tower" after a legendary princess, said to have been confined here after a prophet foretold that she would die from a snakebite. The snake duly appeared from a basket of figs and struck the fatal blow.

Selimiye Barracks ❷

Çeşme-i Kebir Cad, Selimiye. Open Sat, Sun. Visits must be arranged in advance by faxing 0216 310 79 29. Free.

Selim III built these barracks in 1799, but soon after he was killed by insurgents and the barracks burnt down. The present barracks, started in 1828, were used as a military hospital during the Crimean War (1853–6), and Florence Nightingale lived and worked in the northeast tower from 1854. Her rooms are now a museum. They contain their original furniture and the lamp from which she gained the epitaph "Lady with the Lamp".

Haydarpaşa Station ❸

Haydarpaşa İstasyon Cad, Haydarpaşa. Open daily. Free.

This grand station, located on the waterfront next to a tiled jetty, makes an impressive point of arrival or departure in Istanbul. The first Anatolian railway line, built in 1873, ran from here to İznik. As part of his drive to modernize the Ottoman Empire, Abdül Hamit II extended the railway. His German ally, Kaiser Wilhelm II, supplied funds, and in 1898 German engineers started building the new railway lines into the farthest reaches of the Ottoman Empire. New stations were also built. Haydarpaşa, the grandest of these, was completed in 1908. Trains run from here into Asia.

Haydarpaşa Station, terminus for trains arriving from Anatolia

STREET LIFE

RESTAURANTS

Kanaat
Selmanıpak Cad 25, Üsküdar.
Tel 0216 553 37 91. **Cheap**
Busy locanta, serving traditional fare and the best fasulye pilaki (a bean dish).

Moda Park
Moda Cad 265, Moda.
Tel 0216 336 07 95. **Cheap**
Large restaurant with great views of the Sea of Marmara. Excellent fish dishes.

SHOPPING

Tepe Nautilus Shopping Centre
Fatih Cad, Acıbadem.
A huge, ocean-themed shopping mall near Kadıköy ferry port. Includes a cinema.

See p80 for price codes.

BEYOND ISTANBUL

Nothing can beat a boat trip up the Bosphorus, the straits joining the Black Sea and the Sea of Marmara. The shores are lined with handsome wooden villas known as yalıs, graceful mosques and opulent 19th-century palaces, the grander ones with waterfront entrances. Interspersed are former fishing villages, where you will find some of Istanbul's finest clubs and restaurants.

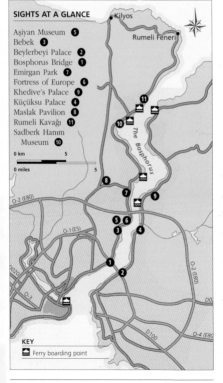

SIGHTS AT A GLANCE

Aşiyan Museum **5**
Bebek **3**
Beylerbeyi Palace **2**
Bosphorus Bridge **1**
Emirgan Park **7**
Fortress of Europe **6**
Khedive's Palace **9**
Küçüksu Palace **4**
Maslak Pavilion **8**
Rumeli Kavağı **11**
Sadberk Hanım Museum **10**

0 km 5
0 miles 5

KEY

Ferry boarding point

◄ Anadolu Hisarı, the Fortress of Asia, on the Asian Bosphorus shore

The Bosphorus suspension bridge between Ortaköy and Beylerbeyi

Bosphorus Bridge ❶

Ortaköy and Beylerbeyi. Free.

The first bridge to be built across the straits, between the districts of Ortaköy and Beylerbeyi, this is the world's ninth longest suspension bridge, with a main span measuring 1,074 m (3,524 ft) long and a clearance of 64 m (210 ft) high. Known also as Atatürk Bridge, it was finished on 29 October 1973, the 50th anniversary of the Turkish Republic.

Beylerbeyi Palace ❷

Çayırbaşı Cad, Asian side. Open Tue, Wed & Fri–Sun. Guided tours. Adm charge.

Designed in the Baroque style by Sarkis Balyan, the palace was built in 1861 as a summer residence for Sultan Abdül Aziz. Empress Eugénie of France visited Beylerbeyi on her way to the opening of the Suez Canal in 1869. Other regal visitors included the Duke and Duchess of Windsor. The palace looks its most attractive from the Bosphorus, from where its two bathing pavilions (for men and women) can best be seen. The most attractive room is the reception hall, which has a pool and fountain.

Bebek ❸

European side.

Bebek is one of the most fashionable villages along the Bosphorus. It is famous for its marzipan, and for the cafés which line its waterfront. Once a favourite location for palaces of Ottoman aristocrats, at the end of the 19th century *caïques* of merrymakers would set off on moonlit cruises from the bay, accompanied by a boat of musicians. The mother of the last Khedive of Egypt, Abbas Hilmi II, was one to host such parties. The khedive used the *yalı* as a summer palace until he was deposed by the British in 1914. Only the Egyptian Consulate remains today. Built in the late 19th century, its steep, mansard roof *yalı* looks French; the railings are draped in Art Nouveau wrought-iron vines.

Ornate landing at the top of the stairs in Beylerbeyi Palace

The Fortress of Europe, built by Mehmet the Conqueror

Küçüksu Palace ④

Küçüksu Cad, Asian side. Open Tue, Wed, Fri–Sun. Adm charge.

Marble-fronted Küçüksu Palace has one of the prettiest façades on the Bosphorus, with a curving double staircase leading from the waterside. Built by court architect Nikogos Balyan for Sultan Abdül Mecit I's entourage, and completed in 1856, the sultan complained that it was too plain and demanded more ornamentation, including his monogram engraved on the façade. Later it was further embellished. The rooms are arranged in Ottoman style, with a large central salon opening on to four corner rooms. There are fine carpets from Hereke and Bohemian chandeliers.

Aşiyan Museum ⑤

Aşiyan Yolu, European side. Open Tue–Sat. Adm charge.

Aşiyan, or bird's nest, is the former home and museum of Tevfik Fikret (1867–1915), one of Turkey's leading poets. The wooden mansion is a fine example of Turkish vernacular architecture. The views from its upper-storey balcony are stunning.

Fortress of Europe ⑥

Yahya Kemal Cad, European side. Open Thu–Tue. Adm charge.

This Fortress was built by Mehmet the Conqueror in 1452 as his first step in the conquest of Constantinople. Situated at the narrowest point of the Bosphorus, the fortress controlled a major Byzantine supply route. Across the straits is Anadolu Hisarı, or the Fortress of Asia, which was built in the 14th century by Beyazıt I. The Fortress of Europe's layout was planned by Mehmet himself. While his grand vizier and two other viziers were each responsible for the building of one of the three great towers, the sultan took charge of the walls. In the spirit of competition which evolved, the fortress was completed in four months. It was garrisoned by the sultan's elite fighting corps. After they had sunk a Venetian vessel, this route to Constantinople was cut off. Following the conquest of the city, the fortress lost its importance as a military base and was used as a prison. The structure was restored in 1953, and today hosts open-air theatre performances.

Hot-house plants in the conservatory at Maslak Pavilions

Emirgan Park ❼

Emirgan Sahil Yolu, European
side. Open daily. Adm charge for
vehicles.

Emirgan Park has famous
tulip gardens, at their finest
for the annual Tulip Festival
in April. Tulips originally
grew wild on the Asian
steppes and were first prop-
agated on a large scale in
Holland. In the late 19th
century Sultan Abdül Aziz
gave the park to İsmail Paşa,
the Egyptian Khedive. It has
three pavilions: the Swiss-
style Sarı Köşk, the Neo-
Classical Beyaz Köşk and
the Ottoman Pembe Köşk.

Maslak Pavilions ❽

Büyükdere Cad, Maslak. Open
Tue, Wed & Fri–Sun. Free.

A royal hunting lodge and
country residence, much
prized for its glorious views,
the pavilions were built in
the early and mid-19th
century, when the focus of
Istanbul court life moved
from the city centre to the
sultans' lavish estates on the
Bosphorus. The buildings

are thought to date mainly
from the reign of Abdül Aziz
(1861–76) who gave them to
his son Abdül Hamit. The
latter personally crafted the
balustrades of the beautiful
central staircase in the Kasr-ı
Hümayun (the Pavilion of
the Sultan). The pavilion's
lounge retains an Oriental
feel, with a low sofa and a
central coal-burning brazier.
Behind the small but elegant
Mabeyn-i Hümayun (the
Private Apartments) is a
large conservatory full of
camellias, ferns and banana
plants. The Paşalar Dairesi
(the Apartments of the Paşa)
are located at the other side
of the complex.

Khedive's Palace

Khedive's Palace ❾

Hidiv Kasrı Yolu 32, Çubuklu. Open daily. Free.

Built in 1907 by the last khedive (the hereditary viceroy of Egypt), Abbas Hilmi II, to designs by the Italian architect Delfo Seminati, this summer palace is one of the most striking buildings of its era. Its tower is an imposing landmark on the Bosphorus. Most impressive of all is the round entrance hall. It is entered through Art Nouveau glass doors and features a stained-glass skylight above a central fountain surrounded by eight pairs of columns.

Attic vase, Sadberk Hanım Museum

Sadberk Hanım Museum ❿

Piyasa Cad 25–29, Büyükdere. Open Thu–Tue. Adm charge.

Based in two archetypal early 20th-century *yalis*, the Sadberk Hanım Museum opened in 1981. Azaryan Yali, a four-storey mansion, contains some fine ethnographic artifacts collected by Sadberk Hanım, to whom the museum is dedicated. Some tableaux depict 19th-century Ottoman society, including a henna party and a circumcision bed. There is also a display of infinitely delicate *oya*, Turkish embroideries. The other *yali*, Sevgi Gönül Win, houses archaeological items from the late Neolithic period (5400 BC) to the Ottoman era, including Assyrian cuneiform tablets, Phrygian metalwork and Greek pottery.

Rumeli Kavağı ⓫

European shore.

From its harbour this pretty village has great views of the wild, rocky shores on the approach to the Black Sea. On the hill above are the scant remains of a 12th-century castle, İmros Kalesi, built by Manuel I Comnenus to guard his customs point. Further up the Bosphorus, the road leads Altın Kum beach, popular with locals.

The fishing village of Rumeli Kavağı, on the upper Bosphorus

Getting Around Istanbul

It is possible to walk between most major sights in Istanbul, and central areas are well served by an expanding system of metro and tram lines. Buses and dolmuşes provide city-wide transport, but it is best to avoid the busy rush hours.

Taxis

Taxi cabs are fairly cheap and the fare is metered. It is 50 per cent higher at night, and a toll is added for crossing the Bosphorus Bridge. They are bright yellow, with the word "taksi" on a sign on the roof, and can be hailed in the street. Most taxi drivers do not speak much English, if any. It is best to carry a map and to have the name of your destination written down.

Dolmuşes

Dolmuşes are shared taxis with fixed routes, cheaper than regular taxis and more frequent than buses. Drivers usually wait until every seat is taken. Starting and end points are marked. Ranks display a blue sign with a black "D" on a white background. A main centre for dolmuşes is Taksim.

Bus

Different coloured buses operate, but they ply similar routes and charge equal fares. You can buy tickets at main bus centres, newsagents, kiosks and from private vendors. Crossing the Bosphorus bridges incurs a double fare. A hop-on-hop-off service covers all the main sights.

The Tramway

The clean, modern tram is the fastest way to get around the city. You purchase a token which operates the turnstile (or use an AKBİL pass). To board a tram, buy a flat-fare token from the booth (gişe) near the platform, and put it into the slot at the top of the platform steps. Trams run every 5 minutes.

Nostalgic tram travelling along İstiklâl Caddesi in Beyoğlu

The Nostalgic Tram

Nostaljik Tramvay (nostalgic tram) covers a distance of just over 1 km (just under 1 mile) along İstiklâl Caddesi from Tünel to Taksim Square. The trams are the original early 20th-century vehicles, and the ticket collectors wear period costume. Tickets can be purchased from kiosks at either end of the line.

The Metro

The metro system is clean and well run, with air-conditioned carriages, and has two lines: from Taksim to Levent, and from Aksaray to the airport. A new section linking the two opens in 2009. Wait to board near the middle of the platform.

Metro sign

The AKBİL Travel Pass

This "smart" token can be bought and loaded with units at public transport ticket offices. It is valid on the metro, tram, ferries and sea buses and city buses.

A sea bus catamaran, Istanbul's fastest form of water transport

Ferries

Ferries called *vapur* cross the Bosphorus and the Golden Horn. The main terminus on the European side is at Eminönü. It serves Üsküdar, Kadıköy and trips up the Bosphorus (labelled Boğaz Hattı). Ferries up the Golden Horn (Haliç Hattı) run from the west side of the Galata Bridge. Karaköy is the terminus for boats to Haydarpaşa and Kadıköy. A number of private motor boats also cross the Bosphorus and the Golden Horn.

Sea Buses

These modern catamarans (*deniz otobüsleri*) are considerably faster and more comfortable than ferries, but cost three times as much.

The Bosphorus Trip

Daily ferry excursions run up the Bosphorus. Arrive early as they get crowded in the summer. You can break your journey once on the same ticket.

Buying Boat Tickets

For ferries and sea buses, you need to buy a flat-fare jeton from the booth (*gişe*) at the pier or alternatively from one of the unofficial street vendors who sit nearby and sell them at slightly higher prices. These jetons can be used for all local journeys.

TRAVEL INFORMATION

Tourist Information Office
Tel 0212 518 18 02
Metro and Tramway Information
Tel 0212 568 99 70
Ferry Information
Tel 0212 444 44 36
Sea Buses
Tel 0212 444 44 36

Survival Guide

Istanbul is as safe as any other European city, and visitors rarely encounter violence or theft. If you are on your own, avoid suburbs bordering the city walls, especially at night. In the event of any trouble, contact the Tourist Police.

SAFETY

Police

There are several police forces in Turkey, wearing different uniforms. The Security Police *(Emniyet Polisi)* is the main force in Istanbul. Its officers wear dark blue uniforms and caps, and pale blue shirts. The Tourist Police *(Turizm Polisi)* is a branch of the Emniyet Polisi. Most officers speak one or two European languages. The Tourist Police station in Sultanahmet, opposite the Basilica Cistern, is open 24 hours a day, and has an English-Turkish translator available Mon–Fri, 8:30am–5pm.

Theft and loss of property

Property left on public transport can be reclaimed from IETT Buses. Check also with the Tourist Police because lost items are often handed in to them by those who found them. Unfortunately, the level of petty crime has risen, especially picking pockets and purse snatching, so be aware and take sensible precautions. Take extra care in crowded areas and at night.

Turkish Security Police

Typical sign for a pharmacy in Istanbul

MEDICAL TREATMENT

The first port of call with a minor complaint should be a pharmacy *(eczane)*. Pharmacists are well trained and many speak some English. Outside opening hours, a note in the window of a pharmacy will give the address of the local *nöbetçi eczane* (duty pharmacist). There are excellent free public clinics *(poliklinik)* all over Istanbul, offering treatment for minor ailments. General practitioners are called *tıbbi doktor*. Their clinics, above shops in all the main shopping areas, are advertised by prominent signs outside. The Turkish health system has public and private hospitals. Private hospitals are well equipped and have highly professional staff (the doctors are also more likely to speak English and other languages), and are more comfortable than the state hospitals. The state health system has few reciprocal agreements with other countries. You are strongly recommended to take out both travel and medical insurance.

MONEY

Banks
Most banks are open from 9am–noon and 1:30–6pm. The İş Bankası at Atatürk airport is open 24 hours. Many foreign banks can be found in Turkey with familiar logos and services.

Credit Cards and ATM Machines
Credit cards and many debit cards are widely accepted. Some smaller establishments may not accept cards in winter even if they do so in summer.

Currency
The currency is known as the New Turkish Lira (YTL, or TRY). The banknotes come in six denominations: 500 YTL, 100 YTL, 50 YTL, 20 YTL, 10 YTL and 5 YTL. All the notes display the head of Atatürk on one side, with Turkish sights on the reverse. The nickel coins are known as *kuruş*.

Exchange Offices
Exchange offices include Para Döviz in the Grand Bazaar, Bamka Döviz in Taksim and Çetin Döviz on İstiklâl Caddesi. These will offer a better exchange rate than banks and are open for longer hours and also on Saturdays.

Cash dispenser with instructions

COMMUNICATIONS

Public Telephones
To make calls from public call boxes, post offices or "boutiques" buy a phonecard. Available from post offices and from street sellers and kiosks, they have a concealed scratch-off code that allows you to make local and international calls from any landline.

Mobile Phones
Turkey's main mobile phone operator, Türkcell, has roaming agreements with 180 countries, so that most people can use their mobile as they would at home. The main exception is North America. You can also buy prepaid SIM cards from all mobile operators.

Internet Access
Istanbul has many internet cafés, most with broadband. Broadband and Wifi are now also found in many better hotels and pensions.

Postal Services
Stamps are available only from post offices and PTT kiosks. Letter boxes are yellow and labelled PTT. They may display these signs: *Şehiriçi* (local), *Yurtiçi* (domestic) and *Yurtdışı* (international). Air mail is *uçak ile*, registered *kayıtlı* and recorded delivery APS.

EMERGENCY NUMBERS

Ambulance 112
Night Ambulance
(0212) 247 07 81
International Hospital
(0212) 663 30 00
Police 155
Tourist Police
(0212) 527 45 03

Index

Acknowledgments

Dorling Kindersley would like to thank the following people whose help and assistance contributed to the preparation of this book.

Design and Editorial
Publisher Douglas Amrine
Publishing Manager Vivien Antwi
Managing Art Editors Sunita Gahir, Mabel Chan
Cartography Casper Morris
Editorial Alex Farrel, Pollyanna Poulter
Production Controller Shane Higgins
Picture Research Ellen Root
DTP Natasha Lu
Jacket Design Tessa Bindloss
Revisions Sebnem Atilgan, Helen Partington, Conrad Van Dyk, Dora Whitaker

Picture Credits
Every effort has been made to trace the copyright holders, and we apologize in advance for any omissions. We would be pleased to insert appropriate acknowledgements in any subsequent edition of this publication.

t = top; tl = top left; tc = top centre; tr = top right; cla = centre tree left above; ca = centre above; cra = centre right above; cl = centre left; c = centre; cr = centre right; clb = centre left below; cb = centre below; crb = centre right below; bl = bottom left; b = bottom; bc = bottom centre; br = bottom right.

The Publishers are grateful to the following individuals, companies and picture libraries for permission to reproduce their photographs:

ALAMY IMAGES: Kevin Lang 6b; Ali Kabas 9cr, 25b; Visual Arts Library (London) 19tr; Robert Fried 19bc; Craig Lovell/Eagle Visions Photography 17b; Danita Delimont 18b.

PERA PALAS: 44tl.

JACKET
Front – ALAMY IMAGES: Hugh Sitton Photography.
Spine – DK IMAGES: Tony Souter b.

All other images
© DORLING KINDERSLEY
For further information see
ww.DKimages.com

Price Codes are for a three-course meal per person including tax, service and half a bottle of house wine.
Cheap under US $20
Moderate US $20–$40
Expensive US $40 or more

SPECIAL EDITIONS OF DK TRAVEL GUIDES

DK Travel Guides can be purchased in bulk quantities at discounted prices for use in promotions or as premiums. We are also able to offer special editions and personalized jackets, corporate imprints, and excerpts from all of our books, tailored specifically to meet your own needs.

To find out more, please contact:
(in the United States) **SpecialSales@dk.com**
(UK) **travelspecialsales@uk.dk.com**
(in Canada) DK Special Sales at **general@tourmaline.ca**
(in Australia) **business.develop ment@pearson.com.au**

Phrase Book

In Emergency

Call the police!	*Polis çağrın!*	po-**lees** chah-**rubn**
Fire!	*Yangın!*	yan-**guhn**
Where is the nearest telephone?	*En yakın telefon* **nerede?**	en ya-**kuhn** teb-leb-**fon** **neb**-reb-deb
Where is the nearest hospital?	*En yakın hastane* **nerede?**	en ya-**kuhn** has-ta-**neb** **neb**-reb-deb
Help!	**İmdat!**	eem-**dat**
Stop!	**Dur!**	door
Call a doctor.	**Bir doktor** **çağrın.**	beer dok-**tor** **chah**-rubn
Call an ambulance.	**Bir ambulans** **çağrın!**	beer am-boo-**lans** **chab**-rubn
Call the police.	**Polis çağrın!**	po-**lees** chab-rubn

Communication Essentials

Yes	**Evet**	eb-**vet**
No	**Hayır**	b-**'eye'**-ubr
Please	**Lütfen**	lewt-fen
Thank you	**Teşekkür ederim**	teb-shek-**kewr** **eb**-deb-reem
Excuse me	**Affedersiniz**	af-feb-der-see-neez
Hello	**Merhaba**	mer-ba-ba
Good bye	**Hoşça kalın**	bosb-**cha ka-lubn**
Here	**Burada**	boo-ra-da
There	**Şurada**	**sboo**-ra-da
What?	**Ne?**	neb?
When?	**Ne zaman?**	neb **za-man**?
Why?	**Neden?**	neb-**den**?
Where?	**Nerede?**	**neb**-reb-deb?

Useful Phrases

How are you?	**Nasılsınız?**	na-subl-sub-nubz
I'm fine.	**İyiyim**	ee-**yee**-yeem
That's fine.	**Tamam.**	ta-**mam**
Where is/are ...?	**... nerede?**	... **neb**-reb-deb
Do you speak English?	**İngilizce biliyor** **musunuz?**	een-gee-**leez**-jeb bee-**lee**-yor moo-soo-nooz?
I don't understand	**Anlamıyorum**	an-**la**-mub-yo-room
Can you help me?	**Bana yardım** **edebilir misiniz?**	ba-na yar-**dubm** eb-deb-bee-**leer** mee-see-neez?

Useful Words

big	**büyük**	bew-**yewk**
small	**küçük**	kew-**chewk**
hot	**sıcak**	sub-**jak**
cold	**soğuk**	sob-**ook**
good/well	**iyi**	ee-**yee**
open	**açık**	a-**chubk**
closed	**kapalı**	ka-pa-**lub**
left	**sol**	sol
right	**sağ**	saa
straight on	**doğru**	dob-**roo**